Are We There Yet?

Sexuality, the Church, and the Road to Transformation

By Drew Berryessa

Unless otherwise indicated, all Scripture quotations are from the ESV® Bible (The Holy Bible, English Standard Version®), copyright © 2001 by Crossway, a publishing ministry of Good News Publishers. Used by permission. All rights reserved

AMP: Scripture quotations taken from the Amplified® Bible (AMP), Copyright © 2015 by The Lockman Foundation Used by permission. www.Lockman.org

MSG: Scripture taken from *The Message*. Copyright © 1993, 1994, 1995, 1996, 2000, 2001, 2002. Used by permission of NavPress Publishing Group.

NIV: THE HOLY BIBLE, NEW INTERNATIONAL VERSION®, NIV® Copyright © 1973, 1978, 1984, 2011 by Biblica, Inc.® Used by permission. All rights reserved worldwide.

PHILLIPS: The New Testament in Modern English by J.B Phillips copyright © 1960, 1972 J. B. Phillips. Administered by The Archbishops' Council of the Church of England. Used by Permission.

A Living Letter Ministries
P.O. Box 8544
Medford, OR 97501
www.alivingletter.org

ISBN: 1719325219

Printed in the United States of America

Dedication

I dedicate this book to my incredible wife, Suzanne. No one in my life has been more a reflection of our Lord to me. You champion me, encourage me, correct me, inspire me, believe in me, and ground me. Your patience and grace over the years is one of the most significant reasons I have a story to write at all. I love you!

Acknowledgements

I am indebted to so many for their influence and support over the years which are reflected in the pages of this book. It would take too long to name them all. There are, however, some who today stand out among the rest:

James and Amy – You embraced a broken young man and infused value and hope into his hopeless heart. You are forever the instruments God used to change the trajectory of my life.

Lance and Rebekah - With over two decades of friendship under our belts, you two have been some of the safest, most loyal, and invaluable people in my life. Thank you for loving me through my most dysfunctional seasons. You two are the best!

Jason and Amy – From counselors, to mentors, to friends, your contributions to my life, health, and maturity will only accurately be measured or fully know in eternity. I love you both and can never thank you enough!

Ryan and Kate – For seeing "more" in me and making space and opportunity for my "more", from day one. Suz and I are unbelievably blessed to walk life alongside you both.

Matt and Will – It takes a lot of love, and a lot of guts to walk this road together. Thank you for having both. We love you guys.

Anna – Thank you for offering your substantial gifts, and incredible presence to help bring this book out of me. You are a gift!

Contents

Introduction

Picture a family road trip: A car is driving The Loneliest Road in America, the stretch of Highway 50 running interminably through open Nevada desert. The kids are restless in the backseat. Wa-a-a-a-y in the forward distance, a hint of a mountain range is visible. But it never seems to get closer. The kids keep leaning forward, asking their parents, "Are we there yet?"

When it comes to talking about sexual identity, you might feel like a kid in the back seat. Or you might feel like the parent driving. But if you are on this journey for any length of time, you are going to wonder, "Are we there yet?"

Neither the corporate Body of Christ nor its individual members have done a very good job at talking about—let alone engaging with—issues of sexual identity. Those issues have been my focus for the last twenty years. For the first five of those years, I was fighting to overcome same-sex attraction, and for the last fifteen years, I've been involved in what has been called ex-gay ministry. Not the label I'd choose, but hey.

After enduring my own struggles and then spending years helping people through theirs, I have come to believe there is no formula for sexual orientation—or for transformation. There is no 1 + 1 = homosexual. And there is no 1 + 1 = transformed. Unfortunately, our culture likes step-by-step formulas and easy answers for our problems. And our Church culture does, too. I see this almost every time a parent or family member comes to me and says, "My loved one thinks they are gay. What do I need to do to fix them or convince them they are wrong?" This desire for a quick fix is also evident in the conclusions people draw, like, "My son thinks he's gay. He's just deceived." As if something so complex as sexual orientation or sexual identity can be narrowed down to a single wrong belief.

I would be dishonoring the hundreds of men and women I've talked with over the years if I reduced their struggle to a simple equation or a nice and pithy sentence.

I will say this: Human beings are magnificently complex. The development of sexual orientation and desire is no different. Even the American Psychological Association recognizes the complexity of sexual orientation development:

> There is no consensus among scientists about the exact reasons that an individual develops a heterosexual, bisexual, gay or lesbian orientation. Although much research has examined the possible genetic, hormonal, developmental, social and cultural influences on sexual orientation, no findings have emerged that permit scientists to conclude that sexual orientation is determined by any particular factor or factors. Many think that nature and nurture both play complex roles; most people experience little or no sense of choice about their sexual orientation.[1]

But the lack of a formula doesn't mean we can't address this struggle holistically and effectively. This book is my attempt to do that—and to look at transformation as the process it is—transformation of our identity and

---

[1] "Sexual Orientation & Homosexuality," *Monitor on Psychology, American Psychological Foundation,* www.apa.org/topics/lgbt/orientation.aspx.

transformation of the way we are able to engage with people who share differing beliefs about identity.

Maybe, one day soon, we'll finally get there—whatever *there* looks like. Meanwhile, as we keep asking or listening to the question, "Are we there yet?" let's try to journey together with grace and love.

Chapter 1

The Defining Moments of Drew's Development

As a kid, did you ever think: "When I grow up, I want to be a controversial pastor in what people will call ex-gay ministry?" Me neither.

It's been interesting. And if you're willing to hear my story, I think you might be as surprised as I was at what God can do.

Let me start at the beginning.

I am a child of the '80s. This was the paleolithic—I mean—pre-World-Wide-Web era. Pre-Netflix. To watch a movie, you either went to the movie theater or drove to your local video rental store and checked out a VHS, a videocassette tape. Yes, tape. So, humor me. Let's think of this chapter as a VHS tape called *The Defining Moments of Drew's Development*. Ready?

Play

I was born in 1977, the year the original *Star Wars* movie came out. Cue a timeline reaching into the galaxies, beginning with a low-res image of a lightsaber and then moving on to 1980s icons like trapper keepers, acid-washed jeans, big hair, and parachute pants. Picture one or more of those icons on a short kid with big ears, fuzzy hair, and a very sensitive disposition. That was me.

In many ways, the early years of my life felt like happy reruns of *The Wonder Years*. My parents were both extremely hard workers. My dad worked at the county sheriff's office, and my mom worked in a call center for a regional telecommunications company. I grew up as one of three boys: my older brother, my identical twin brother, and me. We spent hours playing with Star Wars action figures in our sandbox. (I am sure there is at least one Luke Skywalker still buried in that backyard somewhere.)

Our family eventually moved to the country, where my brothers and I had more space to play, chickens to chase, and a dog and cats to enjoy. We seemed like your typical, middle-American Christian folks who followed the advice of *Focus on the Family* and attended church.

In fact, some of my earliest memories were of church. I was about four years old when I first accepted Christ as my Savior. This was a big decision for me. I was fresh from the guilt of stealing a cookie from the cookie jar, or something just as dastardly, and I felt my need for a savior, stat, so I asked Jesus to save me.

Later, at seven or eight, I remember making my way to the church altar during a Sunday service. The pastor had invited people to come up and confess our failures or sins to the Lord and receive forgiveness. I walked forward and knelt and prayed. I don't remember what I confessed, but I remember how free and light I felt when I got up. I walked back to my family, and when I reached my seat, I felt so relieved and met by God in my confession that I began thinking, "What else can I confess?" I must have gone back to that altar at least two more times in that service. I am sure some of the adults didn't understand why a grade school kid was running back and forth to the altar during a more sober part of the service—especially since every time I came back, I was smiling. I am sure I appeared disrespectful on the outside, but inside I was being met by my Father, and I felt His joy in receiving me.

A parallel reality was growing up right along with me in the '80s, and that was the awareness of the gay community and the fear of the emerging AIDS crisis. Even as a child, I began to notice a disproportionate focus on these issues in the Church. As HIV and AIDS began to enter national awareness, they were met with plenty of fear and judgment, especially since they became associated with the gay community. I often heard preachers or Christian leaders directly tie the reality of AIDS to God's judgment on the gay community.

I can sum up in one word what most of the Church thought of people who identified as gay: *abomination*. In fact, I can still hear a particular pastor quoting Leviticus 18:22, with all the fire and brimstone tones that come with such a verse: "You shall not lie with a male as with a woman; it is an abomination." In pastoral discourse that followed, I repeatedly heard, "Homosexuality is a sin." Further, a very distinct conclusion was drawn about those who experience such attraction; the sinners themselves were the abominations.

Pause

Now, don't hear me wrong. I fully agree with Scripture that the *act* of homosexual sex is sin. But that isn't what the pastors were saying decades ago—or even what so many pastors say today. This may seem like simple semantics, but I assure you, there is a huge difference between calling an *act* an abomination versus calling the *person* doing the act an abomination.

Play

I should mention that, at this point in my childhood, I would not have identified my same-sex struggle. I was hearing this stuff when I was in kindergarten through second grade, long before any sexual attraction began to emerge in my consciousness, and long before I even had a concept of what sex was—but not before I felt a deep longing to connect with other boys and men emotionally and relationally. That was already well on my radar. But I would be dishonest if I said that those first longings were sexual. I *can* honestly say I already felt different than a lot of boys my age. I was more sensitive and emotional—and maybe a bit more dramatic. Good thing I've outgrown that (sarcastic voiceover here).

Another big element was also informing my awareness of homosexuality, or rather the homosexual individual: Uncle Paul. One of my earliest memories is of my third or fourth birthday. I can't remember if Uncle Paul had given me the scratch-and-sniff sticker book about Hansel and Gretel, or if he just happened to be there and was reading it to us, but I have a distinct memory of him scratching and sniffing the gingerbread sticker. Funny what you remember. (I'm pretty sure the book did *not* include a scratch-and-sniff sticker for the part where Hansel and Gretel shoved the witch in the oven.)

Anyway, Uncle Paul was a friendly and funny and enjoyable presence in my life, and he put a human face to a community that received a lot of vitriol and judgement from the Church. I loved my uncle Paul, and whatever he was, he didn't seem like an abomination. And even though my family was a part of a conservative, legalistic Christian community, they did not reject him, either. Uncle Paul was part of our family, and we still loved him. He was a human being, and he was a good one. I just couldn't classify him in the same terms the Church was saying God used to describe him.

All that to say, in my childhood, I received an incredibly mixed bag of messages about homosexuality and the homosexual person. In my young heart, I was already having feelings of disconnection, longings to connect with peers of my same gender, and questions about what that might mean.

And then the soundtrack of my life shifted from a peppy pop song in C major to a synthesizer lament in F minor. I didn't see it coming. To me, nothing in my family seemed out of the ordinary, let alone ready to implode. It wasn't until the summer between my third- and fourth-grade school years that the brokenness of my family surfaced. That was the summer my parents announced their divorce.

Pause

Just so you know, this is not going to be a "This is how my parents failed me" chapter. Let me say right now that no matter what happened after my parents divorced, I have a wonderful relationship with both of them today. I am now a parent myself, trying to raise three healthy, functional daughters. I can tell you that the amount of grace and mercy I have toward my parents increases dramatically the older my own children get.

Play

My parents both had families of origin with brokenness and dysfunction, and though understanding that has given me a great deal of perspective about why they made the choices they did during that painful season when our family separated, I still emerged with deficits and wounds. I know it was never my parents' intention, but we kids were collateral damage. Divorce is always traumatic, whether it is civil or a crap circus. Unfortunately, our family experienced the latter.

There's a reason God values relationship so highly. He speaks to us and frames understanding of who He is and how we are related to Him most consistently through the analogy of family. He gives us the analogy of Himself as the Bridegroom and us, His people, as the Bride. He identifies us as His adopted children, and He constantly refers to Himself as Father. These are all familial terms. So, it would make sense that family should be the greatest context for us to understand His heart and intentions; the healthy family structure is vital to us as human beings. But when God's intention for your family is disrupted, you're going to emerge with wounds, deficits, or scars. That has certainly been true for me.

Honestly, the hardest part of sharing my testimony is uncovering the hurts from that season of my parents' divorce. Both my dad and my mom have so much good in them, and I hate the thought of them being reduced to their mistakes or brokenness during an impossibly hard process. Still, I know that sharing some of the overarching dynamics, if not the details, is vital to understanding the nature of my struggle and how God has healed and continues to heal me.

When my parents divorced, my relationship with my father was severely disrupted. In fact, between my fourth-grade and eighth-grade years, my connection with my dad went from sporadic to practically nonexistent. I was a young boy, and I needed my dad's presence. But that wasn't something I got to have. When we finally did reconnect, the summer before my ninth-grade year, we had each built up so much pain and distrust that we spent the greater part of twenty years rebuilding our connection.

Relationship with my mom was also severely damaged. Again, there is no benefit in explaining the details, except to say that the circumstances and choices each of my parents made during those years left deep fissures in security and trust within my siblings and me.

Sometimes parents do everything right and still end up with broken and dysfunctional kids. And some parents are a hot mess, yet their kids turn out amazing despite the dysfunction of the parents. All that to say, regardless of what went down with my parents, I don't blame them for my struggles. At the same time, I recognize that I grew up feeling a great lack of love and identity and an excess of insecurity.

One of the constant battles of my life has been feeling like I didn't measure up as a guy—that I severely lacked masculinity. Practically speaking, my family did not encourage or emphasize a lot of culturally "masculine" things—either before my parents divorced or after. I didn't have any interest in sports. No interest in hunting. No interest in guns. No interest in so many of the things my peers valued. Now, that was not because I was gay. My family just didn't invest in those "masculine" things, so I had no interest in learning them, and therefore, I had no experience in using them as a platform to relate to other guys who *did* invest in them. Let me reiterate: Not being on the football team or wielding a hunting rifle doesn't make a guy gay, nor does it make him less masculine. It did, however, make it difficult for me to relate to other guys who valued those things, and it made it difficult for me to see myself as masculine when I compared myself to them.

As my parents' divorce unfolded, another trauma sucker-punched my nine-year-old heart. This wound came from a place that was supposed to be safe: church. My church did not handle my parents' divorce with grace or mercy—at all. That was evident in little ways, but it is the big way I'd like to share.

My greatest early rejection from my Christian community came in the most seemingly innocuous of church events: a potluck. Yes, a potluck was the backdrop for one of the most powerfully wounding and influential moments of my life and spiritual journey. To be specific, it was a Thanksgiving-ish potluck my church held one evening at the nearby junior high cafeteria. My mom brought my brothers and me to this event at the encouragement of the senior pastor. It was a suggestion along the lines of: "Have some food and fellowship to ease the pain of the complete upheaval of your lives and family." Kind of a tall order for Tater Tot casserole, but we were desperate.

Unfortunately, fellowship and love were not served with the side dishes.

Every time I think of that event, the details rush in with an immediacy, even all these years later. How no one talked to us. How no one made eye contact with us. How people spread out at their tables so there was no room for our family. When we finally found a seat on the edge of the gathering, it felt like a large, repellant force field extended around us—people kept at least ten feet away at all times.

I remember feeling so confused, vulnerable, and exposed. What was happening? This church had taught me that Jesus loved me. I assumed that meant His people would love me, too. And I used to feel they *did* love me. But no more. I remember turning to ask my mom what was going on. When I did, I saw that the front of her blouse was wet with tears. Silent, abundant tears. And then the air left my lungs.

There is only so much logic and reason that a nine-year-old is capable of. We really don't even have cognitive complexity at that age. And honestly, I don't know how much that would have mattered. Within moments of seeing my mom crying, the realization that we were being rejected because of my parents' divorce crashed on me like a deep, dark wave. I could not have articulated it then, but a transaction happened in my soul at that moment. As an adult, I now know what happened; my soul made an agreement with the enemy. That night, because of the way we were treated, the last safe place in my life was ripped from me.

Remember, only a year or so before this, I had first felt the freedom and joy of confession at church. I had run to pray at the altar, had confessed, had felt the safe arms of the Father as He forgave me. I had felt at home. But the night of the potluck, I just felt like I'd been had.

Somewhere in my soul a new "truth" arose. It went something like this: "If you share your brokenness or sin in church, people will judge and reject you."

Eventually, the senior pastor came over to us and quietly said, "I think it would be best if you all went home. You are upsetting people."

At that moment in my heart, the image of my loving, heavenly Father turned into the image of a few of His unloving people. After that, I did not risk honesty with Christians again for over a decade.

The rest of my childhood after that potluck felt like a void: a gaping lack of love, connection, or identity. I felt empty, unlovable, and alone.

Proverbs 27:7 tells us: "One who is full loathes honey, but to one who is hungry everything bitter is sweet." It is a human reality that when you're well-fed, you're not as vulnerable to being driven by your hunger. But when you're malnourished and starving—when you haven't had a meal in a long time—anything is better than nothing.

Have you ever eaten fast food? If you have ever pulled up to a drive-through, rolled down your car window, and received a meal that came in a paper bag, then you have proven the truth of Proverbs 27:7. Because, let's face it, fast food is not a healthy choice. We don't look at the gleaming neon signs on the roadside, beacons of convenience and artificial flavors, and think, "This is a wise choice." Nope.

When I pull into the drive-through and place my order through the speaker box, I am not thinking about things that nourish me. All I'm thinking is, "I'm hungry!" I'm not concerned with my health or well-being; I'm driven by my hunger. That is a super dangerous place to be! When we reach a point where we are driven by our hunger, it will lead to a destructive end. I think of Paul's warning in Philippians 3:17–21:

> Brothers, join in imitating me, and keep your eyes on those who walk according to the example you have in us. For many, of whom I have often told you and now tell you even with tears, walk as enemies of the cross of Christ. *Their end is destruction, their god is their belly, and they glory in their shame, with minds set on earthly things.* But our citizenship is in heaven, and from it we await a Savior, the Lord Jesus Christ, who will transform our lowly body

to be like his glorious body, by the power that enables him even to subject all things to himself [emphasis mine].

Their god is their belly—their stomach. They are driven by their hunger, desire, and cravings. And to the starving, the bitter thing will seem to taste sweet.

Let me put this another way. Several years back, my wife, Suz, said some of the most dreaded and mortifying words a human being can hear: "Let's go on a juice cleanse." Horror of horrors!

Well, we were on day eight of this cleanse when we had yet another horror—a conundrum of epic proportions. My second-born daughter was still in diapers, and she had run out. No diapers, no bueno. My wife lovingly looked at me and said, "Sweetheart, can you please go to the store and buy more diapers for Liv?"

Now, I'm a good husband, most of the time, so I dutifully went to the store. Do you know, dear reader, how many aisles there are in the store before you reach the diapers? Do you know what is in those aisles? Solid food! Doughnuts! Candy Bars! This is a dangerous place to be on day eight of a juice fast. Let me make a massive understatement: The walk through the aisles of the grocery store that day tested every reserve of self-control that I had developed over my entire life. Conquer life-controlling homosexual struggle? Check. Get through the grocery store on day eight of a juice fast without buying Reese's Peanut Butter Cups? Jesus take the wheel!!!

We are vulnerable when we are starving. Our hunger is elevated to god-like status. And, as one of my heroes, Sy Rogers, often says so insightfully, "True for the body, true for the soul."

Fast forward

I entered my teens starving for love and affection. I believed I did not measure up as a guy, and I struggled to believe I ever would. Because my family was constantly moving around, I had very few friendships. Add to this the influx of adolescent hormones, and you've got a good breeding ground for same-sex struggle. Every non-sexual desire I had to be accepted and loved by other men began to be convoluted with sexual thoughts. This was reinforced by sexual defilement I experienced from multiple sources. And it was cemented by a culture that was constantly drawing the conclusion for me, telling me all of this meant I had an identity that I never asked for and didn't want: gay.

Play

In our culture, if you have a particular set of feelings or temptations and you have some actions or experiences that undergird these feelings, we have a formula to describe you. The inaccurate formula works like this:

Feelings/Attraction + Experience/Behavior = Identity

You can debate where those feelings come from—if they are inborn, biological, or environmental—but once you have confirmed the feelings through action, it seems the die is cast.

Like I said, my religious convictions told me God hated those with a gay identity. Thus, my life from age fourteen to nineteen was marked with an incredible amount of internal turmoil as I attempted to "be good enough" and "spiritual enough" to please God and make up for my innate unacceptability. I secretly struggled with fantasy, masturbation, and fear, yet I wore the mask of a good boy. I prayed every day for God to deliver me from this torment.

But He seemed distant, silent, disappointed, and unwilling to answer that prayer. I was left with few conclusions to draw. Either God didn't exist, didn't hear me, wasn't willing to heal me, wasn't able to heal me—or He didn't have a problem with my sexual orientation.

I understand fully when people draw any of these conclusions. I understand losing faith when you're facing pain and a seemingly unchangeable situation. I understand drawing the conclusion that God is not listening or not caring. I understand the drive to legitimize and justify behavior. But as much as I wrestled and looked into each of these conclusions, I settled into the belief that God was just not willing to heal me, and so I needed to somehow earn that privilege. I need to be good enough, pray hard enough, be pure enough. I felt doomed to chase an ever-moving and elusive target. All through my teenage years, I was constantly reminded of my failure to be good enough. I was constantly reminded of my inability to measure up. I was constantly reminded of my innate unlovability. At age nineteen, I reached a breaking point.

Late at night, in my car on a dark country road, where I was certain no one would overhear me, I had a very honest and loud conversation with God. A lot of pent-up pain and accusation burst from my soul that night. I don't remember everything I said, but I do remember the punchline. It went something like this: "God, I have tried and tried to please you, to be worth your love, to be worth listening to. But all I get is silence and pain. So you know what? If there's a chance I might get to be loved, or feel loved by someone, I am going to take it, because your 'love' sucks. You just leave me empty."

A few months later, when the opportunity to feel relief, to feel accepted, known, wanted, and loved, came—I took it. After all, "to one who is hungry everything bitter is sweet."

I met a guy at church. He was new, and I decided to reach out to him. He seemed like he could use a friend. The true motive of my heart was that I was attracted to him. My motives were driven by my hunger. My god was my stomach—my hunger.

We struck up a friendship. We began spending a lot of time together. I began to fantasize about what might happen if we crossed a line. But that wasn't going to happen. So, I just poured more into our friendship, which quickly became emotionally dependent and exclusive. We began confiding in each other some of our unspoken and hidden struggles, and I learned that not only did he have attractions like me, but he had also been with other guys. Suddenly, my fantasies had potential. After only a few months of "friendship" our relationship became sexual.

Pause

We don't often cop to this in Christian culture, but sin can be really satisfying. I don't know why we don't talk more plainly about this. Even at the Fall we see this reality:

> So when the woman saw that the tree was good for food, and that it was a delight to the eyes, and that the tree was to be desired to make one wise, she took of its fruit and ate, and she also gave some to her husband who was with her, and he ate (Genesis 3:6).

The fruit was good for food, meaning it was delicious and satisfied a hunger. It was delight to the eyes, meaning it was beautiful or visually enticing. And it was desired to make one wise, meaning it gave a knowledge that Adam and Eve were longing for.

I was longing to know acceptance and affection. If each of us were brutally honest, we would admit that sin often satisfies for a season or even just a moment. But that satisfaction doesn't *last*.

We see this truth in Jesus's interaction with the woman at the well in John 4:

> Jesus said to her, "Everyone who drinks this water will be thirsty again. But whoever drinks the water I will give him will never be thirsty again. For my gift will become a spring in the man himself, welling up into eternal life."
>
> The woman said, "Sir, give me this water, so that I may stop being thirsty—and not have to come here to draw water any more!"
>
> "Go and call your husband and then come back here," said Jesus to her.
>
> "I haven't got a husband!" the woman answered. "You are quite right in saying, 'I haven't got a husband'," replied Jesus, "for you have had five husbands and the man you have now is not your husband at all. Yes, you spoke the simple truth when you said that" (John 4:13–18 PHILLIPS).

The woman was trying to satisfy her thirst, not just with physical water but with the temporarily satisfying water of her sexual relationships with six different men. Jesus did not criticize her thirst. He just let her know that the way she was trying to satisfy it would not ultimately work. The satisfaction of sin is not permanent and normally leaves us with a greater thirst.

Play

The first months of my relationship with this guy were exhilarating, satisfying, and medicating. For the first time in my life, I felt fully known, accepted, wanted, and desired. So many longings of my heart began to feel soothed and sated. I began wondering what it might look like to build a life with this guy—maybe get a home together, create memories, love one another.

While all of this was happening, we were hiding the relationship from everyone. It was a small town, and we were both still a part of the church. I was still doing all of my Christian things and was fully involved in a ton of church activities. I was living a double life. Eventually the incongruity and deception of my life began filling me with fear. The Holy Spirit began gently and lovingly confronting my heart. I remember one day the Lord simply and quietly spoke to my heart, "Drew, if this relationship is so good and right, why are you hiding it?"

Sin promises to satisfy, and it does. It also enslaves. Soon the relationship that I had found so much satisfaction and relief in became a prison of shame and desperation. I began to feel conviction and dissatisfaction. But the overwhelming fear became leaving the chains of my slavery; they were both painful and comforting. Bitter and sweet.

There is a definite struggle on the journey from slavery to freedom. We have a tendency to want to hold on to the satisfaction and satiation that slavery can offer. When we are facing the decision to leave the comforts of slavery and walk headlong into the desert and the leanness of fighting for freedom, we can make the most ridiculous trades. A passage in Numbers 11 gives an insight to this. The children of Israel

19

had left Egypt, and they were on their way to the Promised Land, but they were not there yet:

> Now the rabble that was among them had a strong craving. And the people of Israel also wept again and said, "Oh that we had meat to eat! We remember the fish we ate in Egypt that cost nothing, the cucumbers, the melons, the leeks, the onions, and the garlic. But now our strength is dried up, and there is nothing at all but this manna to look at" (Numbers 11:4–6).

I'd like to highlight two things here. One: in that moment, Israel's appetite was tempting them to give up freedom for produce. Not a great trade. Two: God's provision, although sustaining our needs, is not guaranteed to satiate all our desires or tastes. When I was confronted with the pull to surrender my sinful relationship, I did not disagree with the Holy Spirit that the relationship was broken and outside of God's will and design. What I was unwilling to do was go back into the desert of obedience. I had known those hunger pains for so long that I had no desire to experience them again. So, I found myself stuck as a slave to the satisfaction of slavery, which was becoming more and more bitter every day.

Eventually, I reached a moment of decision and left the relationship. That is another story for another chapter.

By sharing some of these moments and seasons in my life, I hope to show how someone can find themselves in this place of entanglement. However, like I said in the introduction, there is no 1+1= homosexual. I have met so many people over the years and have heard hundreds of stories about the vulnerabilities, defilements, abuses, agreements, and environments that led people into their struggle or into adopting a gay, trans, or other sexual identity. Though each of us has a unique storyline—a unique thread—we are all part of the tapestry of humanity.

What would it look like if the Church began to look beyond the *what* to see the *why* in the lives of people struggling with sexuality? The *what* is the exterior brokenness—the symptoms. Simply addressing the *what* is not going to lead broken people to freedom. It certainly didn't for me! If we want to be truly free to live fully as God intends us to live, and if we want to help others get to freedom as well, then we have to get past the *what* to see the *why*.

Rewind

If we want to help others get to freedom as well, then we have to get past the *what* to see the *why*.

Play

This is *so* important. After all, it is easy to make judgments about behavior—that's judging a tree by its fruit, right? And yes, it's important to look at the external fruit in a person's life. But here's another angle to that metaphor; a pear tree is going to produce pears, no matter how many times you pick off the pears and pray for apples. In the same way, when we focus simply on sin management or the exterior *what*, all we are doing is picking the fruit, hoping next season will bring a different harvest.

The *why* is our motivation toward sin. Motivations vary, but more often than not, they are rooted in legitimate needs that have been affected or exaggerated by offenses, abuses, or starvation. That was the case with me.

Somewhere along the way, our God-given needs for love, identity, and affirmation were not met as God intended.

This leaves us vulnerable and hungry. For the person seeking healing, knowing and addressing the motivations of the heart is the only path to healing. Although it is important to address our behavior, that alone does not lead us to healing.

God desires *complete* healing for His children. Through my own journey, I have seen how God was more concerned with proving Himself faithful to address and meet the needs reflected in my behavior than He was with removing the behavior itself. Psalm 103:5 and Psalm 37:4 both allude to the fact that God cares about the deep desires of our hearts, and He purposes to meet those needs in good ways. In fact, I believe God did not answer my consistent prayer that He would take away my homosexual desires so that He could lead me to discover what was really behind these desires and then meet them in His perfect way.

When we take the time to look past people's sin to see the motivations and, consequently, discern their need, we are being imitators of Christ. Remember in John 4, when we see Christ interacting with the Samaritan woman at a well? Simply telling her to stop her bad behavior would not have done much to heal her or address her true thirst. Instead, Christ pointed her to living water that would truly satisfy her. How gracious of God not to condemn her for her actions but rather to address her true desires and meet the true longings of her heart.

I believe we are called to do the same. How desperate is the need for this kind of understanding and compassion toward our brothers and sisters in Christ and the broken and searching in the world around us! How many people do you think are bound by sinful thoughts and actions, and yet have no real understanding of the deep-seated longing in their hearts that keeps them bound? Let us, as the hands and feet of Jesus, look past the *what* to see the *why*. Let us—in love, compassion, truth, and wisdom—address the needs represented in the *why*. If we do, I believe we will see our churches, homes, and relationships become places of great healing for the sexually broken.

Stop

Alrighty, then. Now you know where I'm coming from. And now we're ready to look for the true *why* that will shape the *what*.

Chapter 2

What Identity Are You Claiming?

Why should we be concerned to divide up things into "classes" and "families"? We get away from all this tangle of guess-work, when once the Eternal Word speaks to us. From Him alone all creation has but one voice for us; He, who is its origin, is also its interpreter. Without Him, nobody can understand it, or form a true judgment about it. Until all things become One for you, traced to One source and seen in One act of vision, you cannot find anchorage for the heart, or rest calmly in God.[2]

—Thomas à Kempis, The Imitation of Christ

Today, that passage feels like a weighty layer of blankets: heavy but also secure and warm. The concept of identity has come up in multiple conversations recently. It is a touchy topic for a lot of people, particularly when the issue of sexual attraction gets mixed in. But while sitting at the auto shop waiting for my Jeep battery to be replaced, drinking crappy coffee, smelling tires, and reading *The Imitation of Christ* (I know, perfect environment for deep

---

[2] Thomas à Kempis, *The Imitation of Christ*, Ronald Knox and Michael Oakley, Trans. (Ignatius: 2005), 28–29.

spiritual meditation), this passage reminded me of arguments I had with Christ concerning my own identity.

It was December of 1996. I was sitting in my bedroom, feeling defiled and hopeless. I was feeling the conviction that I needed to end the secret relationship I had with another guy from my church. Neither of us were admitting that we were gay, or that we were boyfriends, but we were spending most of our free time together, spending nights together, engaging in sexual acts, and even looking at apartments to share. In one sense, we were in complete denial, but in another, we were beginning to build a life together. I was deeply conflicted and confused. And in that bedroom, somewhere in the middle of the night, probably after once again looking at porn or fantasizing and masturbating (sorry for the grittiness of all of this, but hey, it's the truth), the voice of the Lord once again butted its way into my heart and asked me to surrender.

I distinctly remember telling God that I was gay. That was significant, because it was the first time I had dared to say it. His voice persisted in calling me to surrender. Somewhere in the tug-o-war that night, my soul slipped slightly over the line toward Him, and I began to give in.

In *Mere Christianity*, C.S. Lewis writes these words, as if spoken by the Lord:

> "Give me all of you!!! I don't want so much of your time, so much of your talents and money, and so much of your work. I want YOU!!! ALL OF YOU!! I have not come to torment or frustrate the natural man or woman, but to KILL IT! No half measures will do. I don't want to only prune a branch here and a branch there; rather I want the whole tree out! Hand it over to me, the whole outfit, all of your desires, all of your wants and wishes and dreams.

Turn them ALL over to me, give yourself to me and I will make of you a new self—in my image. Give me yourself and in exchange I will give you Myself. My will, shall become your will. My heart shall become your heart."[3]

This was the gist of my fight. God wanted all of me, including my own understanding of my identity. I do not have the proper perspective to identify myself. My perception is too polluted. It is defiled by the hateful, hurtful words people have spoken over me and that I have spoken over myself. It is tainted by my insecure, striving heart—begging to feel valued, seen, and esteemed. It is too influenced by the illicit pleasures of sexual sin and defiled imagination. It is too limited to what I can achieve or conjure or understand. It is fickle. None of us can trust ourselves to accurately say who we are. That is why Kempis's words felt so soothing to me this morning and reminded me of that sweet, terrifying moment of surrender. I needed the one who made my soul—who holds my eternity secure, who is the only accurate interpreter and the only source of hope that I have—to be the only one with the authority to tell me who I am.

And what did He say to me in that moment in my bedroom when my lips spoke an identity that my affections, my relationship, and sexuality seemed to reveal? Well, if I were to write it all down, I would certainly burst into tears, and I don't think the other patrons of the auto shop where I am currently writing this would know what to do with that hot mess. What I will dare to write is that the Lord spoke tenderly and softly to my heart of my value as His son, of His plans and intentions for me as a man, and that when He

---

[3] C.S. Lewis, *Mere Christianity: An Anniversary Edition of the Three Books, the Case for Christianity, Christian Behaviour, and Beyond Personality*, Walter Hooper, Ed. (Macmillan, 1981), 153.

looked at me, He did not see the word *gay*. He told me to agree with Him. To stop resisting Him. He told me to trust Him.

OK, now I *am* crying. Crap.

Here is the bottom line. I do not share this experience to criticize anyone who claims a gay identity. Especially if Christ is not your Lord and Savior. If you are not connected to the One who made you and formed you, then I cannot and will not criticize the way you understand your identity. I will only invite you to investigate the claim that Christ is the source of all life, that He is Savior and Lord. That He loves you indescribably and is ready and waiting to have a similar conversation with you. For my brothers and sisters in Christ who claim a gay identity in addition to their Christianity, I do not share my experience to criticize your understanding of who you are. I fully understand how you would come to that conclusion. What I would simply like to share with you is the wonderful rest my soul experienced when I surrendered my right to define myself in those terms.

For all other readers: We all have our baggage and lists of experiences and struggles that the enemy of our souls uses, probably on a daily basis, to rob us of the only true identity that matters—our identity as sons and daughters of God.

May we all take a moment right now to quiet our minds and let the One who made us whisper tenderly and quietly to our aching hearts, telling us who we really are.

***

I've never liked labels. Maybe it was because words have always carried such weight for me. With words we can bless, and we can curse. We can build up and we can tear down.

The Scripture says the power of life and death are in the tongue; literally, words can make the difference between life and death. When you consider the number of people who choose to end their lives because of the hateful, hurtful words spoken to, about, or over them, it is staggering. Words, especially in the form of labels, have power.

Moment of vulnerability here. I mentioned that I had really big ears as a kid. Huge. Epic, in fact. At least that's what I believed because of the litany of insults I received as a kindergartner. A boy in my class once asked me, "Why don't you fly home, Dumbo?" The memory is visceral: where I was sitting, the time of day, and the feeling of my face going red. Today, I recognize that kind of insult is small potatoes. But the fact that I so vividly remember those words and that my self-perception was altered for years to come because of them proves the point: Words have power.

I can also clearly remember the first time I heard the label *abomination*, as I wrote about in the first chapter. It was at church, and the pastor had just finished quoting Leviticus 18:22. I remember where the pew was in relation to the stage. I remember, of all things, the pastor's haircut. I remember the feeling of my face going red. I remember how hopeless I felt. And I remember that, for years to come, my self-perception was altered when words created a label and that label stuck to me.

It is an incredibly demoralizing thing to feel condemnation for something that you feel you have absolutely no choice or control over.

I am happy to report that over the years a few very important transformations have happened in my life. First, I realized that my ears are appropriately proportioned to the size of my head. Second, I discovered that I was not helpless or hopeless regarding my same-sex attraction. Neither of these shifts happened overnight. Both required a certain amount of self-acceptance to get through the rough periods, but just like most things in life, they had more to do with self-perception than a fixed reality. Time, growth, and perspective shifts helped immensely. If I were to try to stretch the analogy any further, I am sure it would crumble, since big ears and same-sex struggle are *vastly* different animals, so I will end it here and get to the real point: The words we speak or accept as true have incredible power over us.

The Book of James gives us a great reminder about the power of the tongue:

> So also the tongue is a small member, yet it boasts of great things. How great a forest is set ablaze by such a small fire! And the tongue is a fire, a world of unrighteousness. The tongue is set among our members, staining the whole body, setting on fire the entire course of life, and set on fire by hell (James 3:5–6).

Strong stuff.

I can't recall how many times I was labeled as gay. Whether it was an explicit remark made by some school-yard bully or a more passive insinuation made by a culture that interpreted my internal struggle for me via a TV show or movie, it was continual and countless. Added to that was the condemnation spoken over that identity—from derogatory jokes made by friends in youth group to the hatred and disdain that dripped from the mouths of people in church as they talked about "those people." The words I heard were clear: I was gay, and I was hated.

The odd thing is, I never spoke the label *gay* over myself until that night talking to God in my bedroom. Call it denial, call me a self-hating gay if you want to go there, but even when I was engaged in a sexual relationship with another guy, I still did not say to myself that I was gay. Oh, I felt gay for sure. And I was certainly acting gay. But I could never actually bring myself to say that I was gay. When I began coming clean with people about my feelings and behavior, my confession was that I was struggling with homosexuality. That was true enough; I was experiencing homosexual attraction, and I was struggling against it. Even when I was years into my personal discipleship and healing process, I still did not really embrace the label of *ex-gay*. I didn't want to be identified for what I wasn't. Why am I making a big deal about this? Because words have power.

As a believer in Jesus, I live with the distinct conviction that the only words I want to accept as part of my identity, or that I want to speak over anyone else, are words that speak truthfully and in accordance with His Word. Practically speaking, this means I need no other labels than those of *redeemed, forgiven, adopted, co-heir with Christ, transformed, made new*, and so forth. Now don't get me wrong: I am adamantly in favor of telling the truth about our struggles and temptations. In no way am I advocating that people deny the reality of a struggle with their sexuality by hiding behind labels that can quickly dissolve into platitudes. But what I *am* saying is that making a struggle into an identity is unhelpful at best and damaging at worst.

I never fully embraced a gay identity, despite very real gay feelings and behavior. Ultimately, I think this served me and my walk with the Lord. Because I never embraced an identity as gay, it was never a fixed and unchangeable reality.

It was a struggle that remained subject not to the lordship of my self-perception or the power of my feelings or history but rather to the lordship of Christ, who had the authority and power to do whatever He wanted with that very real struggle and history.

A thought to consider: Can we, as believers in Christ, choose to temper the words we speak about ourselves and others through the redemptive lens of the gospel? Can we leave the power to speak identity safely in the hands of the only one who has the authority to speak truthfully to who we are? Can we purpose to point people to the hope found in Jesus by the words we speak? Let's do that and see what happens.

Chapter 3

Same-Sex Attraction Is Not Sin

I can almost audibly hear the objections: "Are you telling us to ignore sexual sin and brokenness? God says homosexuality is an abomination! How can you suggest we look past that?"

Let me clarify. I am in no way suggesting we minimize or ignore sexual sin. Sexual sin is incredibly destructive in all its forms. Paul reminds us of the unique aspect of sexual sin in 1 Corinthians 6:18: "Flee from sexual immorality. Every other sin a person commits is outside the body, but the sexually immoral person sins against his own body."

I am not suggesting that we ignore anything, but rather that we look deeper.

Let's start with the difference between *same-sex temptation*, and *same-sex behavior*. How we distinguish these two is *critical* in offering hope, empathy, and ministry to the broken. I'll go back into my own story to illustrate this.

My faith was important to me, and even early in my childhood, I was a little evangelist. I ran around the kindergarten playground asking my classmates, "Do you know Jesus?" And if one of them said, "No," I would yell: "YOU'RE GOING TO HELL!" It's amazing the revivals you can lead on the playground when you threaten kindergartners with eternal damnation. I'm only joking a little bit here. I did actually do this. But I share my sophisticated childhood evangelical strategy to simply say that my faith was important to me. As simple and as immature as it was, it was my faith.

I cared a great deal about what God thought of me. But with the Church's message toward the gay community, with a wonderful uncle I loved who lived a homosexual life, and with the growing insecurities and longings of my own heart to connect with the same sex—by the time I reached early adolescence, my trajectory felt inevitable. To use another pearl of '80s sarcastic slang: "no duh."

The first time I recognized and admitted to myself that I was experiencing same-sex attraction, phrases from sermons I'd heard shoved their way to the front of my mind: "Homosexuality is a sin." "Those people are an abomination!"

My conclusion was: So that's what God thinks of me. What other conclusion could I draw from what I'd been taught? Here I was, a young man undeniably experiencing attraction toward the same sex, and the spiritual authorities in my life were telling me what God thought and felt about people like me: I was an abomination, and the very nature of my attractions and temptations was sin. Imagine if you believed, because of your vulnerability, that God hated you and condemned you at the core of your being. Imagine that He thought you were absolutely abominable and disgusting. Would that make God someone you might want to run to or run *from*?

We as Christians have to take a very blunt, honest, and critical look at the way we communicate about people who struggle with things we don't understand—people who embrace things we understand to be sin.

There are sooooo many problems with classifying *same-sex attraction* as inherently sinful. To be clear, I am not talking about *behavior* here, but the temptation of attraction. Before I get into that, I will say I understand the tendency—and even the logic—that leads people to conflate behavior and temptation. After all, the implications of sexual behavior outside of heterosexuality carry with them a different set of consequences. But the problem is: It's just not theologically correct to classify temptation as sin.

Look at Hebrews 4:15: "For we do not have a high priest who is unable to sympathize with our weaknesses, but one who in every respect has been tempted as we are, yet without sin." The Bible makes it clear that Jesus experienced temptation and yet was without sin.

Now the Bible did not specify the type of temptation Jesus experienced, just that He was tempted in every way. That doesn't necessarily mean He was tempted homosexually, but it certainly doesn't exclude that possibility. If we start classifying one person's temptation as sin and another person's temptation as non-sin, then we start taking authority that isn't ours. God has made it clear in Scripture that temptation is not sin. However, the nature of our temptation, if acted upon, can have very different levels of consequence.

Let me say it one more time. When we start classifying one person's temptation as sin, but another person's temptation as *not* sin, we start normalizing some of the lust and brokenness reflected in those temptations that are deemed more natural or acceptable.

Might I suggest that our temptations can reveal our brokenness?

Just this last year, I read an article by an individual who contrasted homosexual temptation with heterosexual temptation. And I couldn't believe what I was reading. He was praising the virtue of heterosexual lust versus homosexual lust, as if lust was a goal.

As the father of three daughters I cherish and protect, I will say that lusting after women is not more virtuous than lusting after men. All forms of lust are broken, distorted, and selfish. If you lust after the opposite sex, it does not mean you are holier or better; it means your brokenness is different. And if I might be a little cheeky, it also means your brokenness is more relatable to the people making those theological distinctions and judgements. How fortunate for them to not have to contend with those other temptations. But it is a theological overstep, or rather, a load of horse crap, to classify heterosexual temptation as not sin but homosexual temptation as sin simply based on the nature of the temptation.

Again, different temptations can reveal and illuminate different types of brokenness in each of us.

I feel like it's probably important right now to distinguish between lust and attraction. They are, in fact, very different and distinct things. Lust is a passionate or overmastering desire or craving. Attraction isn't even necessarily sexual in nature. Let me give you this example.

I frequently speak across the country, and to illustrate this point, I like to specifically ask a question of the men who attend my teachings. By and large, most groups I speak to are not full of individuals struggling with same-sex attraction, but rather people who are trying to understand how to respond, minister, or relate to those who do struggle. So, the majority of the men I speak to do not necessarily find other men sexually attractive.

To this group of men, I frequently say, "Gentleman, let me ask you a question. And please be honest with me. Do you know the difference visually between a very good-looking man and a very unattractive man? I'm not gonna be cruel here and name names or give descriptions, but humor me. Can we admit that there are some men who look very attractive and some who don't?" When I ask this question, there's always a bit of awkwardness. Men don't usually have the permission to admit this reality. Women sure do. In fact, the women usually giggle at the scenario, watching the discomfort of the men in the room as they sheepishly admit that, in fact, some men are better looking than others. They laugh because it is not uncommon for women to compliment or openly admire other women without it being weird or sexual; women have permission to recognize aesthetic beauty without it threatening their sexuality. On the other hand, men in this culture haven't had the same permission or freedom to recognize attractiveness in another man without it being uncomfortable or even implying same-sex attraction. But recognizing aesthetic beauty or attractiveness can have nothing to do with sex. It has to do with admiration, and sometimes comparison, and the fact that God created us with eyes and with aesthetic appreciation. Again, this doesn't necessarily have to do with lust or sex.

Think about it: Advertisers do not use unattractive men to advertise men's products. They use men who are handsome, who are fit, who are admirable looking, who have characteristics or qualities that are appealing to other men. And this is because men want to emulate these other men in the ads. It's not about sex. It's about admiration. When I bring this up to the men in these crowds, I see the subtle recognition: "It's true. I don't want to buy shaving cream from a man who looks slovenly. I want to buy it from the man with a strong, distinct jaw line and handsome features—even though I have four chins!" (OK, that might be me speaking.)

It's also not just the physical that were attracted to. Why do we choose the friendships we choose? Why do we hang out with the people we hang out with? Because we see admirable qualities in their personalities—qualities we are attracted to. We place ourselves in the lives of people we want to emulate. Generally speaking, we relate to people who have qualities we are attracted to. That's attraction. It can have nothing to do with sexuality and everything to do with admiration.

Now, it's absolutely true that our attractions can be based on a number of different things. For example, I might be drawn to friends who have a particular characteristic or quality I feel like I lack. I wanted to be confident, and I was often drawn in friendship to people who were confident. Maybe, subconsciously, I thought that by virtue of friendship and proximity to those friends, some of their confidence would rub off on me. Also, I'm drawn to people who are intelligent. Part of my draw toward them is that I want to learn from them. Sometimes I've been attracted to people based on shared values and beliefs; there's a sense of comradery in knowing that we understand each other, and we don't have to explain ourselves. Those are all forms of attraction.

I didn't have any of this understanding as a young man. I thought every pull I felt toward someone of the same sex was homosexual in nature, and thus, sin. The nature of my attractions always led me back to somewhere broken. And because of my brokenness, I assumed every attraction was wrong or sinful, because I had been told that temptation and attraction were sin. How very unfair, compassionless, and incredibly unhelpful.

Whether we want to admit it or not, our temptations reveal something about us. Temptation is like a dashboard light on a car, telling us that something is wrong or out of order. In that regard, temptation can be quite instructive. When I'm tempted to eat fast food, something that I have an abundance of experience with, it reveals to me that I'm hungry. It reveals to me that I need to eat and that my body needs fuel. When I am tempted, I have a couple of options. If I judge myself on the nature of what feels attractive, that attraction is based on the taste and appetite I have cultivated; it's based on what's available to me or what I've trained myself to hunger for. Alternately, I can choose to look at the temptation as a messenger telling me that something is out of order or unaddressed in my life. I can then choose to meet that need or address that disorder rightly or wrongly. Again, this is not sinful, it just *is*.

Scripture is clear about temptation. James 1:14–16 puts it this way:

> A man must not say when he is tempted, "God is tempting me." For God has no dealings with evil, and does not himself tempt anyone. No, a man's temptation is due to the pull of his own inward desires, which can be enormously attractive. His own desire takes hold of him, and that produces sin. And sin in the long run means death—make no mistake about that, brothers of mine! (PHILLIPS).

Scripturally, temptation itself is not sin, but when tempting "desire takes hold," the result is sin and death.

This is *so* important for every believer to understand! I would even say that for those who struggle with same-sex attraction and other forms of sexual brokenness, it is absolutely essential to understand this distinction. Believing that temptation itself condemns you leaves you in a constant state of defeat and despair. In my own struggle, interpreting every temptation of same-sex attraction as sin left me feeling demoralized and condemned. That interpretation robbed me of the opportunity to use my will to make healthier choices to address the needs behind the inward desires.

In my own struggle with same-sex attraction, I was attracted to different types of guys. Sometimes they were physically fit and full of confidence and seemed to have life all figured out. I was not fit, was full of self-deprecation, and did not have anything figured out. I viewed myself through a very critical lens, physically and emotionally. Instead of understanding that my temptation or attraction was a messenger—a dashboard light to inform my heart—I fixated on the things I found attractive and allowed myself to lust after the men who possessed the characteristics I felt I lacked. My temptation took hold of me and produced the sin of lust. This process was no different for me than it is for anybody else, regardless of the object of attraction or lust.

I wish I could tell you that I first learned to see my same-sex temptation from a more biblical and practical perspective with the help of a pastor or theologian. But nope. Instead, the door of understanding this stuff was opened to me by a friend, an ordinary guy with no theological training or experience with same-sex temptation. He is a good and godly friend, and ours is one of my oldest and longest friendships—now spanning over twenty years. I admire his character, his intelligence, his faithfulness, and his integrity. We are kind of like an odd couple in friendship: I'm short, pale, and less physically impressive, whereas he is a tall, dark, and handsome personal trainer and college basketball player. On paper, we don't match up, but I don't think I've ever had a more faithful, more helpful, or more patient friend. God gave him an incredible ability to speak directly to lies I believed about my value and identity and the patience to endure some of my most dysfunctional and persistent attitudes of insecurity. Really, he is a saint, and I don't believe I would be who I am today without his friendship.

I will never forget the day we went shopping in a sporting goods store. I don't remember what we were there to get, but as we were walking through the aisles, I noticed a label attached to some swim trunks, which featured a handsome, fit, shirtless guy. Of course, the tapes started playing in my head. Thoughts like, "Well, since I clearly notice the attractive guy, I am clearly guilty of homosexual attraction, and therefore, I am clearly a hopeless, abominable, wretch." That was the gist of the monologue that always ran through my head when I noticed an attractive guy in real life, TV, print, or where ever. Mind you, I wasn't fantasizing about the guy on the label. I just simply saw the image, recognized that the model was attractive, and BOOM! Condemnation.

In the middle of my internal shame cycle, I suddenly heard my friend's voice—the voice of a man who has no shred of homosexual attraction in his soul at all—saying something like, "Wow, that guy is super fit."

I blinked. He was referring to the same label I had just seen.

I looked at him and said, "What? You noticed that?"

Until that moment, I had thought guys who didn't struggle with same-sex attraction only saw other guys like, I don't know, Lego figures, or blobs, or indistinct shapes, but somehow, I had made an agreement in my mind that no straight man could see what I saw when noticing an attractive man.

In a nonchalant tone, my friend said, "Of course I did. I have eyes! He's in great shape. I would love to be that ripped."

I stood there dumbfounded. Now granted, my friend did not have to go through the same mental gymnastics I did to understand or interpret what he saw, and certainly he did not have the same vulnerabilities I did toward being tempted to sexualize another guy. But that conversation dispelled a lie I didn't know I was believing. A lie that said even noticing or recognizing attractiveness or physical beauty in another guy made me somehow broken or guilty. Turns out, I just had eyes. Go figure.

Now, this realization did not make all my struggles go away—not by a long shot. By that point in my life, I had cultivated a lustful, covetous, sinful response to attraction and temptation. I still had to go through a long process of cultivating a new response. I still had to learn to take my thoughts captive and make them obedient to Christ and His call to holiness and integrity. But what that sporting-goods-store revelation *did* do was begin to equalize the playing field. I could evaluate what was going on in my heart and mind when I saw someone attractive without leaping to a place of condemnation and defeat. I could understand that just recognizing attractiveness is not the same as lust, and it did not automatically mean I was sexually attracted to the person. That might sound simplistic or confusing to some of you, but I can assure you that for me this was a game changer. I no longer had to feel condemned if I noticed a handsome man in the room, and not feeling condemned somehow took away a large portion of temptation's power.

Just because you see someone who might be attractive does not mean you're obligated to lust after them or sexually objectify them. Attraction itself does not mean you are guilty of any sin. Maybe you just have eyes.

When I began to see that simply recognizing attractiveness wasn't a sin—and really wasn't even homosexual—I began to wrestle with the question, *When does attraction turn to lust?*

This is one of the central questions anyone attempting to be holy in their heart and mind has to contend with. If you grow up feeling wretched for temptation or attraction, the stakes are even higher when determining where you draw a line of moral responsibility. It's incredibly important for those who struggle with sexual identity issues to be able to settle this question in their hearts. Otherwise, how can they differentiate between vulnerability and something they have more responsibility for?

That's another reason why classifying the state of being attracted to the same sex as inherently sinful is so frustrating to me. That distinction leaves absolutely no room for people to make morally responsible choices in response to their vulnerability. If you're guilty at the mere hint of attraction, where do you go from there but toward more guilt? I can't tell you how many times I've counseled people—and not just people with same-sex attraction but also people struggling with all sorts of lust—who feel that once they cross a particular line of guilt, they might as well go further because, if they're already guilty of sinning, they might as well get a little enjoyment.

If you classify the state of attraction as sin, what's your motivation to be more holy? How do you talk to someone else or go for pastoral support or counseling if you already know they're going to judge you and condemn you for the nature of your temptation? This distinction between attraction or temptation and lust is extremely important if our goal is discipleship and redemption. Space for victory exists in the moment of temptation—but not if we classify temptation as sin.

So back to the question: *When does temptation turn into lust?* (Remember, *lust* is a passionate or overmastering desire or craving.) I think I was attending Portland Fellowship, a ministry for those dealing with same-sex attraction, when I heard a teaching specifically on lust. It was probably one of the more gracious teachings I've ever heard on the topic. The basic pastoral instruction was not to create a universal hardline for when temptation becomes lust. The idea goes like this: The moment you become aware that you are dwelling on or cultivating your temptation to the place of fantasy or objectification, that is the precise moment when you have a decision to make. I think this approach is very gracious—as in: full of grace—and is more like how the Holy Spirit interacts with us.

The Holy Spirit knows our immaturity. He knows our vulnerabilities. He knows our history and all the things we have wrongly cultivated in our lives. Sometimes, you don't even know your thought pattern is wrong because it's simply what you have cultivated for most of a lifetime. I think of those who experienced sexual abuse or defilement as children. They may not even know that their later actions or behaviors are defiling, because such things shaped their development. In some people's lives, defilement can feel normative.

But then the Holy Spirit begins giving us insight or conviction beyond our experience and inclinations. A moment comes when you know you can choose to proceed or back out.

It's humbling to admit this, but early in my process of discipleship through same-sex attraction, my moment of conviction was very far into some pretty sinful behavior. I had cultivated a life full of fantasy and masturbation. It had become very easy to enter that cycle of lust without a second thought. When I first began confronting this behavior, I was often already into the act of fantasy and lust before feeling a twinge of conviction. And God met me there.

I was already engaging in sinful behavior, and yes, ultimately God's goal for me would be to overcome that to the point where I wouldn't be involved in that sinful junk at all. But maturity and strength and consistency all take time. It took me a while before I began feeling that nudge of conviction *before* my thoughts crossed into the territory of lust, and I believe God had mercy for me in the season leading up to that. I'm not saying He approved of my actions or that I wasn't guilty of sinful thoughts and behavior, but God knew I was immature and broken, and He was leading me to a place of holiness and maturity with grace and patience for my imperfection in the process. God is a good Father, and He knows what it takes for us to learn and grow.

This is in no way a passive process. God calls us to obey His voice. He calls us to take responsibility for our thoughts and actions, and He takes into account our immaturity and our brokenness as we grow.

Repentance always felt to me like something that happens if you're caught and confronted. I used to engage with God from a place of personal disgust or deep shame, normally after having committed some sin or having dwelt on a temptation. This would leave me feeling broken and defiled. I would feel bad, but it would never lead me to change or transform. Ultimately, repentance is transformation. Repentance is not about feeling bad for what you've done; that is regret or remorse. And for extra measure, confession is not repentance. Neither is agreeing that your behavior is sinful. Repentance is actually moving in a new direction of obedience and holiness. Repentance is not a passive process. It is not feeling bad. It is conviction that leads to active choices as God pursues our hearts.

Two of the most challenging verses for me in this process are in 2 Corinthians and Romans 2:

> For godly grief produces a repentance that leads to salvation without regret, whereas worldly grief produces death (2 Corinthians 7:10).

> Or do you presume on the riches of his kindness and forbearance and patience, not knowing that God's kindness is meant to lead you to repentance? (Romans 2:4).

It seems we in the Church like to quote one or the other, but we don't like to wrestle with the truth in both.

Yes, contrition and grief are essential to repentance. We have to be confronted with the wrong that we are doing. But let's not forget that this alone will not produce godly sorrow. Satan himself will tell us what we are doing is wrong, and he will keep us hopelessly chained to it! Knowing that fantasy, pornography, my gay relationship, and masturbation were sins did not lead me to repentance. Without knowing the patient, gracious, forbearing kindness of God, knowing my sin was wrong only kept me in a place of misery and condemnation. It was in response to experiencing the love of God that true repentance began to happen in my life.

Contrition and grief came as a response to holy love! I've been broken open by the gentleness of God. I've been broken open by His approachability. I've been broken open by His patience with me. I've been broken open by His willingness to engage with me about things I believed He would never ever be willing to hear. All this made me want to run *toward* God. It made me want to pursue Him back.

A shift began to happen when I realized I wasn't guilty or condemned if a thought simply entered my mind. When a thought came, I had an opportunity to engage with the Holy Spirit and my own soul about it. This understanding brought the Scripture to bear daily:

> For though we walk in the flesh, we are not waging war according to the flesh. For the weapons of our warfare are not of the flesh but have divine power to destroy strongholds. We destroy arguments and every lofty opinion raised against the knowledge of God, and take every thought captive to obey Christ (2 Corinthians 10:3–5).

The process of taking my thoughts captive and bringing them into submission to Jesus, as the Scripture instructs, became a conversation with God—a God who is for me and is unafraid to hear the details of the battle in my heart.

My thoughts began to shift. When a feeling or temptation or attraction arose in my mind, rather than feeling immediately guilty, I began inviting Holy Spirit into the conversation. I would honestly tell Him about what I was thinking or feeling. I would ask Him for wisdom to understand where these thoughts were finding strength or authority.

I found that when I begin having these conversations right at the moment of attraction or temptation, I would discover that my initial thoughts really had nothing to do with sex. Instead, they were rooted in feelings of comparison, envy, or jealousy. Sometimes, a place of wounding or feeling inferior would be the trigger. Often, my initial attractions were simply admiration or appreciation for a guy's characteristics; it wasn't sexual at all. Not all my feelings or attractions were based in brokenness. Sure, there were moments when the lust I had cultivated was the culprit. After all, as the Book of Galatians rightly informs us:

> Do not be deceived: God is not mocked, for whatever one sows, that will he also reap. For the one who sows to his own flesh will from the flesh reap corruption, but the one who sows to the Spirit will from the Spirit reap eternal life (Galatians 6:7–8).

At times, I did reap lust in my heart and mind because I certainly had cultivated it. But it was a lie that every thought was rooted in lust—a lie from the devil to keep me condemned and bound. Not every attraction or temptation was reaping sin. Once I had the freedom to bring these thoughts to the authority of Jesus, He began helping me to discern the difference and to illuminate places in my heart that had been hurt, places that were completely benign, and places that were good and right. After all, there is no sin in admiring what is admirable.

As I brought to the Lord the whole of my thought life, I experienced His love, compassion, wisdom, patience, and kindness. That is when repentance—true repentance—began to happen in my life.

By repentance I don't mean just feeling bad about my sinful thoughts. That's not repentance. Repentance meant turning away from indulging lust *and* turning away from condemning myself over simple moments of attraction. It was a shift from feeling bad and trying to control or repress thoughts in my head (which, of course, never worked) to fully pursuing relationship with God and bringing my thoughts *to Him*.

Scripture instructs us to do just that—to draw near to God in the midst of temptation and to submit ourselves and the whole of our hearts and minds to a God who understands temptation and humanity, and yet is ready to empower us with His grace to resist and stand.

> Or do you suppose it is to no purpose that the Scripture says, "He yearns jealously over the spirit that he has made to dwell in us"? But he gives more grace. Therefore it says, "God opposes the proud but gives grace to the humble." Submit yourselves therefore to God. Resist the devil, and he will flee from you. Draw near to God, and he will draw near to you. Cleanse your hands, you sinners, and purify your hearts, you double-minded (James 4:5–8).

> Since then we have a great high priest who has passed through the heavens, Jesus, the Son of God, let us hold fast our confession. For we do not have a high priest who is unable to sympathize with our weaknesses, but one

who in every respect has been tempted as we are, yet without sin. Let us then with confidence draw near to the throne of grace, that we may receive mercy and find grace to help in time of need (Hebrews 4:14–16).

This interaction became possible for me once I saw that my attractions themselves were not sinful. Realizing they were just temptations gave me permission to interact with the Lord and receive instruction, comfort, and help from Him.

As I took those thoughts captive, I submitted them to Jesus, and He then interpreted and counselled me through them.

***

This next part may seem like a bit of a left turn, but I assure you it applies.

One of my favorite Scripture passages is the story that takes place at the pool of Bethesda. The story goes that whenever an angel stirred the water of the pool, the first person in would be healed. A paralytic man had been lying on his mat by the pool waiting for an opportunity to be healed for *thirty* years. Think about it; this guy's been there for decades. He has no one to help him into the pool, and yet he persists—waiting and waiting and hoping that maybe, someday, by some stroke of fortune or the mercy of God, he will be the first one in the next time the water stirs.

Jesus enters the scene, and within moments of hearing the man's story, He simply asks him, "Do you want to be well?" Jesus then instructs the man to pick up his mat and walk.

I can only imagine what the paralytic felt. He had hoped and dreamed and waited his entire life for healing. And yet I imagine the long wait must have eroded his hope and taken its painful toll on his heart. After all, like Proverbs 13:12 says, "Hope deferred makes the heart sick."

Yet, when Jesus instructed the paralytic to pick up his mat and walk, the man was faced with the decision to either believe Jesus by faith and attempt what moments before was impossible or to believe he did not have the strength to do what Jesus was instructing him to do and remain paralyzed. It takes a lot of faith to dare to do what the paralytic does; he stands up, picks up his mat, and walks.

Every time Jesus healed, we see a similar situation. A miracle happens in the context of a step of faith. Whether Jesus healed the leper, the blind, the lame, or the dead, in every instance, the healing and transformation occurred with faith and obedience. (And if you wonder how faith or obedience could play a role when Jesus raised someone from the dead—there's usually not a whole lot a dead guy can do!—remember that Lazarus' sister, Martha, demonstrated faith and obedience on behalf of her dead brother. Even when we can't manage to eke out faith for ourselves, God is so gracious, He'll use the faith of others.)

In my journey of sexual brokenness, I often felt like the paralytic—just waiting and hoping that, somehow, I would be lucky enough to be healed. For years, I sat on my mat, waiting for someone to throw me into the pool. I was paralyzed by condemnation. I was guilty and defeated before I ever had a chance to stand and walk. I *did* have hope of healing; otherwise, I would have abandoned my faith early on. Jesus cured my paralysis by giving me a chance to be obedient. He gave me a chance to stand up against temptation. He gave me the ability to run to him for grace, discernment, strength, and forgiveness. But again, I wouldn't have even known I could invite Jesus into this process if I hadn't been allowed to believe that my vulnerability, attractions, and temptations were a place for Jesus to interact with me and not automatically a sin to repent of.

So, back to temptation. A proper understanding of temptation leaves believers with a choice of what to do in response to it. Temptation is not sin but a common experience, and God gives us grace to endure and overcome it. That is so hopeful! Believing this helps us move from a victim mindset to a mindset of encouraged strength. A believer who rests in this hope handles temptation differently than one who feels defeated the second an enticing thought assaults his or her mind.

Maybe you feel as though I am preaching to the choir here. Many in the Church would agree with this seemingly self-evident biblical truth concerning temptation in general, yet not so many agree when it comes to temptation of same-sex attraction in particular. Instead, the Church often sees same-sex temptation as a sin to be repented of. That is not biblical. The Scriptures state that sin is produced when a man's desires take hold of him. Empathy and understanding about this can make the difference between hope and despair.

It is not popular to hold this view—believe me, I know. But also believe me when I say that I know from experience that same-sex attraction is partially a symptom of unmet needs. There is nothing to repent of in needing love. There is nothing sinful about wanting to experience affection or companionship. God unapologetically created humanity with relationship in mind. When our desire to connect with the same sex is out of order, even that is not necessarily sin, but rather a symptom of a life impacted by sin and brokenness. The core desire for connection is absolutely *not* sin.

However, if not taken captive and submitted to the lordship of Christ, this desire for connection and love can easily "take hold" of our hearts and minds and lead us into sin.

In order to encourage our brothers and sisters in Christ who struggle with same-sex attraction and any form of sexual brokenness, we must shift how we speak about sexual temptation. Can we speak in a way that doesn't defeat those dealing with these issues before they even have a chance to obey in the midst of temptation? Can we speak the Scriptures back to them, not our own opinions? Can we focus on our common condition—that we are all drawn into sin when we decide to take the place of God by trusting in ourselves to meet our needs and not submitting those needs back to our God who cares for us?

It is not that same-sex attraction is exactly the same as any other sexual temptation; it is not. It reveals a different state of brokenness. It has vastly different implications for what surrendering to Christ might mean long term. It has the capacity to alter our understanding of our identity. It is very weighty and very different. But the nature of the temptation does not make it sin simply because it is different. How I submit any attractions or temptations to the Lord and obey Him in the midst of them is no different from how any Christian should deal with any temptation.

Each of us who calls Christ Lord has a choice. We can either give in to temptation and let our desires take hold of us, or we can obey Christ and hold on to our identity in Him as we forge Christlike character.

Chapter 4

Reaching out to the Homeless and Loveless

Religion that is pure and undefiled before God the Father is this: to visit orphans and widows in their affliction, and to keep oneself unstained from the world.

—James 1:27

I have spent hours contemplating James 1:27. It seems like such a straightforward verse: Take care of the orphans and widows. It is an exhortation that we, as Christians, should take seriously at face value. But we often fail to. For many of us, either because of life stage or lack of proximity, we may not naturally interact with people who fall within our understanding of these two categories. I mean, unless we make an intentional effort to go on a mission trip or pursue becoming a foster or adoptive parent, many of us will rarely engage with orphans. Widows are a different story, though our culture mostly expects them to be cared for by immediate family. Also, we don't have a lot of patience or grace for the grieving. We expect grief to resolve within weeks, and we often move on with our schedules and lives long before those who have lost a spouse.

All this to say, even at face value, we are not great at heeding this command. What is more convicting in this Scripture—and what has captivated me—is the richer meaning and deeper implications in *The Message* paraphrase of it:

Anyone who sets himself up as "religious" by talking a good game is self-deceived. This kind of religion is hot air and only hot air. Real religion, the kind that passes muster before God the Father, is this: Reach out to the homeless and loveless in their plight, and guard against corruption from the godless world (James 1:26–27 MSG).

In this paraphrase, the translator Eugene Peterson exchanges *orphan* and *widow* for two words that force us to look again. The *homeless* and *loveless* are not just people in a far-away third-world country; they may be sitting next to us at church. This I relate to personally.

There was a long season in my life when, although I wasn't technically an orphan, I certainly felt homeless and loveless. The consequences of my parents' divorce were fracturing—and they still pop up from time to time three decades later. I don't share this to criticize my parents in any way. As I mentioned, I now have great relationships with both of them—and my stepparents. However, there was a season in my life when the fallout from the brokenness in my family left me feeling homeless and loveless.

For years, this feeling hung on me like a heavy coat. There was hardly a day that went by when the ache of loneliness or the feeling of worthlessness didn't color my relationships, decisions, or outlook. The one place that this feeling was somewhat alleviated was my church. I felt more at home there than anywhere else, even after that potluck fiasco. That isn't to say that I felt secure there, just that it was the place where I felt the least alone and worthless. For all intents and purposes, it was my safest place. Maybe that is what set me up for the most painful feeling of homeless and loveless I would ever experience, because my guard was down, and I just didn't see it coming.

It was toward the end of high school, and I had gone to the Christmas Eve service at my church. At the time, I was living with my grandma and grandpa. Although my twin brother and I both attended the same church, I am not sure where he was on that evening. We were not sitting together. Since my parents' divorce, no one else in my family had continued attending church, so I was family-less at that particular service. That was fine with me, because I was sitting with friends from the youth group.

It was a beautiful service. The music was stirring, and the sanctuary was lit by candlelight. I felt glad to be there celebrating the birth of Jesus with my church family. Everything was wonderful, safe, and joyous. And then, suddenly, it wasn't.

Nobody did anything wrong. Nobody was hateful or cruel. But near the end of the service, the pastor simply instructed us to move across the sanctuary and gather with our families for a time of devotion and prayer. All my friends disappeared, and I suddenly felt visibly exposed for what I felt I was: homeless and loveless. Nobody meant for me to feel rejected or exposed, but as I watched people join their families, I did.

For a moment, I thought if I didn't move, maybe nobody would notice or see how unloved and worthless I was. That thought quickly passed as I realized hot tears were streaming down my face. I needed to get out of there before I started wailing—which I knew was coming. I could feel it. I had to think fast. If I wanted to maintain any dignity at all, I had to get out of there before I lost control.

I stood up and started walking toward the sanctuary door, calculating my exit even as my heart was breaking; when I got through that door, it would be another twenty yards across the foyer to the main entrance, and then I'd be out in the parking lot. I knew no one would be in the foyer, so I could run once I got there without drawing any attention. Then, when I got outside, I could scream, vomit, cry, wail—everything that I felt rising out of me—without the shame of people seeing me.

Once I made it to the foyer, I began to lose control. I broke into a full sprint as heaving sobs began bursting up from the depths of my soul. My one clear thought was: "Just get to the parking lot! You can fall apart in your car."

Just as I reached the door to the parking lot, thinking I was free, I felt something completely unexpected. It was not a spiritual epiphany. It was not the overwhelming experience of God the Father. Although the Scriptures say He is the Father to the fatherless, and He will never leave us or forsake us, in that moment, His presence was not what I felt.

By the way, Christians often sing well-meaning worship songs with choruses about Jesus being all we need. But God Himself knew that humans would need each other, too. We need family and community. We need people with skin. We need flesh and blood.

When I was almost out the door of that foyer, the strange feeling I felt was the petite hand of a woman named Kathy grabbing my collar and stopping me dead in my tracks.

Gene and Kathy.

When I think about this couple and the many ways they tangibly loved the people in our church, my heart feels like it's going to burst, and my eyes are filling with tears. If I tried to recount all the ways they demonstrated love, hospitality, compassion, and inclusion, I'd have so much material, I'd have to write a whole other book. And if I contacted friends from just the short years of my own youth-group experience at that church, we could collectively fill volumes about this couple.

Gene and Kathy had two kids of their own, Shawn and Julie. Their modest home in Cowiche, WA, was the center of countless youth group hang outs. It was remarkable how many teenagers could fit into their tiny kitchen, consuming endless amounts of chips and dip. It was also amazing how much patience they had for the late nights when dozens of us crammed into their home, noisily playing games or watching movies into the wee hours of the morning. At some point in the night, Gene would simply dismiss himself to go into "the horizontal resting position." He and Kathy never complained about the noise, the mess, or the chaos of all us kids. We knew we were welcome. We were home.

All to say, I shouldn't have been surprised that the hand stopping me at the threshold of despair and the frigid winter night belonged to Kathy. As I turned to face her, I was shocked to realize she must have been running pretty fast to catch me. I was even more shocked to see the tears in her eyes.

"Where are you going?" she asked.

"I don't have a family," I managed to squeak out, still trying to hold myself together.

She looked directly into my eyes with such pain, understanding, compassion, and love. She simply replied, "Yes, you do."

And then she took me by the hand and led me back into the sanctuary, where Gene was sitting with at least ten other "adopted" kids who also needed a family that night.

That passage in James came alive to me: "Real religion, the kind that passes muster before God the Father, is this: Reach out to the homeless and loveless in their plight."

Gene and Kathy were not the only family to love me well through seasons of loneliness, but they certainly were one of the first to teach me true hospitality and how to make room in our families for those whom God might want to love through us. Anyone who has ever felt loved and welcomed by Suz and me should ask the Lord to bless Gene and Kathy. They set a good example for hospitality.

I would like all believers to ask ourselves: How can I tangibly love the loveless and welcome the homeless? We are surrounded by people who may not technically be orphans, but they certainly feel like they are.

On my journey, one of the greatest challenges was the fear of feeling alone and being alone. People leaving homosexuality stand to lose so much to follow Jesus. They may lose their spouse, their identity, their community—everything they have built their lives around. They are very likely going to feel homeless and loveless. That is a heavy weight to bear, and I don't think we are called to bear such weight alone. The Lord has asked His people to see the orphan (homeless) and the widow (loveless) and to care well for them.

I would like to take this a bit further. Let's look at the parable of the sower in the Book of Matthew.

> That same day Jesus went out of the house and sat by the lake. Such large crowds gathered around him that he got into a boat and sat in it, while all the people stood on the shore. Then he told them many things in parables, saying: "A farmer went out to sow his seed. As he was scattering the seed, some fell along the path, and the

birds came and ate it up. Some fell on rocky places, where it did not have much soil. It sprang up quickly, because the soil was shallow. But when the sun came up, the plants were scorched, and they withered because they had no root. Other seed fell among thorns, which grew up and choked the plants. Still other seed fell on good soil, where it produced a crop—a hundred, sixty or thirty times what was sown. Whoever has ears, let them hear" (Matthew 13:1–9 NIV).

Jesus later explains this parable to His disciples:

But blessed are your eyes because they see, and your ears because they hear. For truly I tell you, many prophets and righteous people longed to see what you see but did not see it, and to hear what you hear but did not hear it. Listen then to what the parable of the sower means: When anyone hears the message about the kingdom and does not understand it, the evil one comes and snatches away what was sown in their heart. This is the seed sown along the path. The seed falling on rocky ground refers to someone who hears the word and at once receives it with joy. But since they have no root, they last only a short time. When trouble or persecution comes because of the word, they quickly fall away. The seed falling among the thorns refers to someone who hears the word, but the worries of this life and the deceitfulness of wealth choke the word, making it unfruitful. But the seed falling on good soil refers to someone who hears the word and understands it. This is the one who produces a crop, yielding a hundred, sixty or thirty times what was sown (Matthew 13:16–23 NIV).

We can hear the message of the Kingdom of God and not really get it. If the message has no good place to root in our hearts, persecution and trouble can wipe it out. Or it can be choked out by worries, concerns, or deceitfulness of wealth. Only the seed that falls on good soil—where it is not vulnerable—can begin to root and be nourished and eventually blossom.

I cannot begin to tell you how applicable this passage is to those leaving sexual brokenness. I have seen so many people experience the first blossoming of new life in Christ and freedom from sexual brokenness, but because they could not take root and be nourished in the Church, their new life was choked out. Now I am not talking about church attendance. And I am not talking about becoming a member of a church. I am talking about being brought into the family of faith.

I may have lost some of you here. Stay with me.

The Church as whole could do a far better job of demonstrating family. A good church feels like family. The hallmarks of such a church are love and caring and kindness. Make no mistake: It can be costly and inconvenient to be a family, especially with family members you don't understand or identify with. This is so important that I am going to say it in shouty caps: ANYONE HEALING FROM SEXUAL AND RELATIONAL BROKENNESS NEEDS A COMMUNITY. We need community where we can take root, be protected, and be nourished.

Just about every time I've seen a person go back and embrace sexual brokenness, the reason was either lack of connection in the family of faith or rejecting the family of faith. That rejection can look like dishonesty or avoidance or duplicity or rebellion. It can also look like despair—believing the lies of the enemy who says you are unloveable and rejectable. It can also be straight up fear of vulnerability. When I ran from that sanctuary, my fear and feelings of exposure were pushing me away from the family of faith. I was believing I was rejectable and unlovable.

That Christmas Eve service could have ended as one of the most painful nights of my life. Instead, it ended with a powerful act of love that helped change my life and influenced the way I now minister. I am so glad Kathy was sensitive, saw my pain and loneliness, and chased me down with love.

I encourage you to ask the Holy Spirit to open your eyes to those around you who may need you to chase them down as well. The broken need family. They won't make it alone.

Chapter 5

Confessing the Deep, Dark Secrets

The Book of James says something curious about confession:

> Therefore, confess your sins to one another and pray for one another, that you may be healed. The prayer of a righteous person has great power as it is working (James 5:16).

James tells us to confess our sins to one another so that we are healed. This has proved to be significantly true in my life. So many times, I ran to God asking for His forgiveness and confessing my sin, my weakness, and my perpetual failures. And you know what? He was always faithful to forgive me. But here's the thing; every one of those times I confessed to God, I wasn't healed.

Forgiveness is different from healing. Learning that was harsh. In an earlier chapter, I shared the trauma of the potluck. It was a moment in my history when I begin to believe the enemy's lie that it is unsafe to share your brokenness or sin with people in church, because they will reject you. Such a gross lie. As we used to say, "Grody!"

This lie stands in direct opposition to the spiritual truth we just read in James. And even more frustrating, the lie the enemy was trying to get me to believe was born out of real pain and real experiences of rejection and judgement. My church *did* hurt me. My church *did* reject me and my family because of my parents' divorce. My conclusion was accurate to my experience. And I'm guessing many of you reading this have experienced great rejection, judgment, or pain at the hands of people who call themselves Christians. Yes, the Book of James says we should confess our sins to one another and be healed. But sometimes, the people we are confessing to are jerks—or maybe just people who have never been taught how to handle confession. Maybe we need to raise up more people who create safe places for us to confess. Maybe *we* need to be those people for each other.

Here is my story of confession.

When I was nineteen, I found myself in a gay relationship. I was living a double life; I was involved with a guy but also involved with my church community. I was still on the worship team, still on the youth leadership team, and still fully engaged in my church community—all while hiding this relationship. As I shared before, a lot of my previously unmet heart-needs were being satiated by this relationship, and I was completely unwilling to give it up. I had known loneliness and emptiness so long, and I wasn't ready to go back to them. I was willing to live a divided life instead. For a while.

Inevitably, the allure of the relationship began to wear off, and fear of exposure and discovery begin to creep in. I started feeling trapped between knowing that what I was doing was wrong and not wanting to return to the void I'd felt when trying to do right.

One night, my fog of ambivalence was evaporated by one of the most unlikely sources. It was a Sunday evening, and I had been spending time at our youth minister's house with a group of college students from our church.

I had only known James and Amy for about seven months. They came to our church in May of 1996. I will never forget the day I met them because it was the same day my grandpa died.

I had lived with my grandparents since I was fourteen. Grandpa had been suffering from cancer for years. That morning, I woke to my grandma banging on my door, screaming for me to come and perform CPR on grandpa. The last couple of days had been bad, and we had sensed he would go soon. I ran to his room, got him off his bed and onto the floor, and began to perform CPR. With the first chest compression, I felt his weakened ribs crack and break. I wanted to let my grandpa go. He had suffered for years, and I did not want to try to save him. Mercifully, the firefighters arrived and took over. Grandpa was soon gone. The next few hours of that morning filled with a slow stream of family members gathering to grieve.

I should've been focused on grandpa's passing that day, but the new youth pastors were arriving that afternoon with their U-Haul, and I needed to help with the unloading. Who helps people move a few hours after his father figure dies? An incredibly insecure young man named Drew. I told myself I needed to be at James and Amy's house to unload the U-Haul. I had to make a good impression. I needed to show them that I was valuable and helpful. So, I detached from my grandpa's death and from my family and showed up to schlep boxes like nothing had happened.

Let me say, for the record, that I have an undying love for James and Amy. I can't think of a more providential couple to be in my life in that season. But by the time I met them, I was so broken I didn't have much capacity to receive the love they constantly offered me. I didn't trust them. I wanted to, but I didn't know how.

A few days after they moved in, I met with James to talk with him about youth ministry. I can only imagine what I sounded like. I was an insecure nineteen-year-old kid trying to protect his heart while also trying to win favor with some man I didn't even know. James was incredibly kind, and I didn't quite know how to handle that.

After our meeting, James asked where I was heading to next, and I mentioned that I was going to my grandpa's service. It wasn't really a funeral—more like family hanging out at an Elks Lodge and trying to figure out what to do with our grief. James completely surprised me by asking if he could go with me. I didn't know what to say. I mean, I had only just met the guy, and he really had no reason to care about me at all. The idea that he wanted to come grieve with my family over a man he'd never known was confusing. My I-don't-know-how-to-reply answer was: "Sure fine, if you want to come, be my guest."

James showed up. I remember him weeping with my grandma and hugging her. He was sincere. He was compassionate. He still is. But at the time, I could hardly believe how free he was with his love—and how genuine that love was.

To make a long story short, James and Amy continued to display an approachability and love that was extremely compelling to me. But because I was so broken and still dealing with demons that I dared not share with anyone, I never could believe the love they were offering me was real. I was too familiar with the sting of rejection and abandonment, and I didn't want to open my heart up to them just to experience all that again. If they knew what I struggled with, they would certainly reject me.

As I continued to get to know them and volunteered in their youth ministry, we slowly established a friendship. Several months later, I began engaging in my gay relationship in secret—sure I was hiding it from everyone.

A few months into that relationship, I found myself at James and Amy's house one Sunday night, as I often did. But on this particular night, I planned to go from their house to my "boyfriend's" house—most likely to stay the night with him. An average day in a double life.

When I reached the door to leave, Amy stopped me. "Drew, I need to say something to you."

"Amy, be nice," James said.

"James," she said, "I have to say this." She looked at me, full of compassion, and said, "Drew, you're in sin. We love you, and we see that your sin is killing you. You're not the guy we met when we moved here. We love you. Please repent."

I just stood there in shock and quickly replied, "I don't know what you're talking about."

She just looked at me, full of compassion and said, "Yes, I think you do. Drew, your sin is killing you. Please repent. We love you."

Once again, I replied that I didn't know what she was talking about. And then I bolted.

Notice that Amy did not specify my sin. She did not call it out by name. She simply said that she knew I was in sin, that it was changing me for the worse, that she loved me, and that she wanted me to repent.

When I left that night, I had a tiny hope that maybe she didn't truly know what was going on. But I also had a great big fear that, "Holy crap, God is telling on me!!"

I drove only a few miles down the road before I had to pull over. My first response was anger. I was so angry at God for calling me out. I thought, "How dare you, God! For years I prayed you'd take this struggle away, and you never did. And now that I finally feel loved, now that I have someone who is showing me affection and kindness, *now* you want to address it? *Now* you want to speak? You don't have the right to!"

Pretty soon the anger subsided, and fear set in. "Hey, God, please, please, please don't tell people what I've been doing, OK? Please don't expose me! I'm going to get rejected and kicked out of the church if you do. I can't handle that again! Please God be merciful. Please don't tell people the truth!"

My understanding of our Heavenly Father at that point did not involve a whole lotta love. I saw the Father more like an angry taskmaster or a disappointed boss. I was afraid He was going to shame me into obedience, and I didn't know if I could handle that. And by that point, I don't think I would've been able to handle further exposure. I had already struggled with feelings of suicide and hopelessness, and if God had operated the way I thought He would, I might not be here. I'm so glad I was wrong about Him.

My heart very quickly moved from fear to sadness to resolve. I knew I could not continue my relationship. I knew it was time to let it go. I drove immediately to my "boyfriend's" house as planned, but instead of spending the evening with him, I walked in the door and I said, "I'm sorry. I can't do this anymore. I have sinned against you, I have sinned against God, and have I sinned against myself, and I have to stop." I ended the relationship and left his house.

I'd like to say this confession to God—and even the confessions to myself and this other guy—healed me. But they didn't. God *did* forgive me. God is always faithful to forgive us when we confess.

Still, for the next two years, I lived in constant fear of being exposed. I was deathly afraid of rejection and deathly afraid of exposure. I was certain that God was disappointed with me, I was certain that He was angry at me, and I was certain that He required me to earn His love back. So, I kept hiding my sin and shame, fearing someone would figure out what I had done.

Two years later, I found myself back at James and Amy's house on a Sunday night.

It's funny, the symmetry of it.

I sat on the couch, knowing I needed to confess and that there was no way out of it. I couldn't bear the secrecy anymore. I sat for what felt like hours, crying on the couch, not being able to bring myself to utter the words. James finally opened his Bible. As soon as he began reading, I knew that they knew:

Or do you not know that wrongdoers will not inherit the kingdom of God? Do not be deceived: Neither the sexually immoral nor idolaters nor adulterers nor men who have sex with men nor thieves nor the greedy nor drunkards nor slanderers nor swindlers will inherit the kingdom of God (1 Corinthians 6:9–10 NIV).

He paused when he got to the words "men who have sex with men." When he finished reading the verse, he asked, "Drew, is your sin in this list?"

I just nodded my head. I knew it was all over. I was about to be rejected and judged, shamed and cast out. My history and *everything* I had ever heard the Church speak about homosexuality was about to collide with me, head on. I braced myself as if for a car crash.

Then Amy spoke, so tenderly and mercifully, "Drew, we already knew. We've known for two years." They named the guy, when the relationship started, and when it ended.

I sat there, trying to absorb it. They had known for two years? It honestly didn't compute. They had had two years to reject me, two years to condemn me, two years to make sure I knew what an abomination I was. But for those two years, they had never done anything but show me love, hospitality, and affection. They had invited me into ministry with them, and they had trusted me. None of that made sense when held up against what I had believed would happen if people knew.

I objected incredulously, "There's no way you knew! If you had known, you would have rejected me. If you had known, there's no way you would have loved me like you have! I don't understand! How could you possibly have known?"

James looked at me with tears in his eyes and simply said, "Well, Drew, we love you. We wanted you to feel safe enough with us that you could tell us yourself. We knew you repented, we knew you ended the relationship, and we knew you'd eventually tell us."

I accepted Jesus as my Savior when I was four years old, but I had never experienced His love like this. Sitting on that couch in James and Amy's house, I experienced the kindness and mercy of God in a way that dramatically changed the trajectory of my life.

James then softly asked if I had ever heard the rest of that passage in 1 Corinthians.

"No, I haven't."

I had assumed the verse ended there with condemnation. Every time I had heard that passage spoken in church, no one ever included verse 11:

> And such were some of you. But you were washed, you were sanctified, you were justified in the name of the Lord Jesus Christ and by the Spirit of our God (1 Corinthians 6:11).

I left that night having encountered the love, hope, and presence of Jesus lived out in the patience and understanding of this remarkable couple. Although my moment of confession did not fully heal everything about my same-sex struggles, it did heal me of fear and isolation. It healed the wound created at the infamous potluck.

If, 2,000 years ago, believers who had once been "men who had sex with men" were later washed, justified, and sanctified, then maybe there was hope for me, too.

I ended up confessing to almost fifty people within a week of that confession. I didn't want to live in a prison of fear anymore. With every confession, my heart healed more, and I found that each person I confessed to felt the freedom to share with me secrets the enemy was holding them captive to—the Book of James might have been on to something!

A few months later, in a story too long to tell here, I found myself living in Portland, OR. I know, it's not exactly the city you'd go to if you're trying to recover from homosexuality, but the Lord orchestrated that move, and He has a great sense of humor. Within days of moving there, I met a friend who, because I was no longer ruled by fear of rejection and had the freedom to be honest with my struggle, introduced me to Jason Thompson, a man who had also walked out of homosexuality and helped direct the ministry of Portland Fellowship. Jason would become my mentor and friend—and ultimately, my boss. All this because of confession.

And before I close this chapter, I can't help but point out another bit of symmetry; I don't think it's any coincidence that God used my friend James to help me understand that verse about confession in the Book of James. Like I said, God has a sense of humor.

Chapter 6

Coffee with Room for Cream and a Dash of Apologetics

A few years into my healing process, while I was interning at Portland Fellowship, I worked at a coffee shop in downtown Portland. Working in a coffee shop is no unique experience; plenty of people have taken their turn pulling shots and steaming milk. What made this experience memorable for me was my coworkers.

I was one of only two guys on a staff of mostly women— and all but one of those women were lesbians. Although I was actively involved in a ministry that specifically addressed homosexual orientation, and I had already shared my testimony on national television (thank you Sally Jesse Raphael!), no one at the shop new my testimony or my history. The most my coworkers knew was that I was a Christian. That already felt like enough of an obstacle to work around without bringing the ex-gay baggage into the picture.

I had a keen sense that the Lord had purposed me to be in this coffee shop with these women. I made it my mission to be non-threatening, kind, warm, and relatable. It was easy to do; the women were kind, caring, funny, and interesting. I really enjoyed my time with them. I could also see the ways each of them were wounded. One woman was a pastor's kid, and she had been rejected and condemned for embracing a gay identity. The last thing I wanted to do was threaten any of my coworkers with my testimony or beliefs. I wanted them to get to know me—not to form an opinion of me based on my convictions or my history. So, I remained silent about much of my life and focused on being safe and Christlike.

One afternoon, a month or so after I'd started working at the coffee shop, my permission to remain silent on the topic of homosexuality abruptly ended. It was near the end of my shift. I was in the back room, finishing some paperwork, when one of the women came and stood near the doorway, looking my direction. The best phrase to describe that moment is *pregnant pause*. This is the kind of moment when you know the silence is about to birth something messy and super complicated. I could feel it, almost physically.

"So..." she started, with a tone blending anger, hurt, and tension, "...you're a Christian, right?"

"Oh crap..." was the sanctified version of what immediately flashed through my mind. What's going to be the follow-up to my answer?

I slowly said, "Uhh...yes. Why do you ask?"

With palpable defensiveness, she asked a question that was going to define the tone of my relationship with her and, no doubt, my other lesbian coworkers. "Do you think I am going to hell because I am gay?"

All the air seemed to leave the room. A thousand thoughts ran through my head. Here are a few: "How do I answer this? What do I say? I don't want to offend her! I don't want to push her or the other women away! Oh crap!! What do I say?! Holy Spirit... HELP!!"

Finally, out loud I said: "No... I don't think you are going to hell because you are gay."

She looked at me, both curious and taken back. "You don't?"

"Nope," I said. "You are going to hell for a lot of reasons." And boom goes the dynamite.

It is hard to describe the tension of that moment. I had the stark realization that I was standing in relational quicksand, and the more I might franticly struggle in this moment to get footing, the more I was going to sink.

Again, praying quickly for wisdom, I broke the silent tension. "I am sorry...I think I misspoke."

"You *think*?" she asked sarcastically.

"Yes. I did. You are not going to hell for a *lot* of reasons. But I am sorry to say that I do believe you are headed to hell."

She looked hurt and offended. "OK, if it's not because I am gay, then why do you believe I am going to hell?"

I took another deep breath. "Well, you are Buddhist, right?"

"Yeah, so?"

"Well, in Christian belief, in order to be saved, you need to be reconciled to God the Father by placing your faith in Christ His Son. There is no other way to heaven than to be redeemed through Jesus. Have you placed your faith in Jesus as Savior and Lord?"

"No, I haven't."

"Well," I said, "In Christianity, you don't go to hell if you're heterosexual or homosexual. You go to hell if you are unredeemed."

She processed my words. Of course, I was processing my words as well. This wasn't time for a discussion about the implications of how a relationship with Christ would affect her lifestyle, and this wasn't the time to get into what sanctification is. It was a simple moment and a simple question: *Does being gay send you to hell?*

I watched her soften as her anger dissipated. "OK," she said, "I can accept that answer."

She turned and walked out of the back room. And then I passed out.

Just kidding. I didn't pass out. I took a deep breath and sat with that interaction for a moment. All the years of feeling condemned for my feelings flooded back to me. I remembered asking that question a million times. I remembered hearing numerous Christians condemn people for their homosexuality. I remembered pastors misquoting scriptures, saying: *they* (homosexuals), not *it* (the behavior), were an abomination.

I knew my coworker had believed that I, as a Christian, thought she was going to hell because she was gay, because that is what Christians had told her. But this conversation was bigger than that. Why did she accept my answer? Why did my answer disarm her?

You have to understand that many people who have embraced a gay identity believe fully that their sexual orientation is something they have no choice about and no power to change. And that was true for my coworker. When she asked me if I believed her homosexuality was sending her to hell, what she was really asking was whether I believed in a God who would send her to hell for something she felt like she had no choice about or control over. What kind of God did I believe in if I believed that? Not a kind God. Not a gracious God. Certainly not the God revealed in Jesus. But that portrayal of a cruel God was the one she'd been taught that Christians believe in.

When we approach this topic as believers, our belief is in a redemptive God who can make beauty from ashes, who can heal the lame, who can raise the dead. We know that whatever God calls us to, He equips us for—including obedience to turn from sin and the transformation to live a life beyond what once defined and controlled us.

But we have to remember, people in the LGBTQ community usually do not have these beliefs as their foundation of understanding. They start with the belief that their sexual orientation is unchangeable and unchosen. Their question is: *Why would God send them to hell for something they have no choice about?*

When I told my coworker that not being reconciled to the Father through Jesus is what would send her to hell, I changed the game. She was a Buddhist. She did not believe in Jesus. She made a choice to not believe in Jesus. I might believe she was headed to hell, but at least I believed in a God who would send her there not over something she had no choice about, but rather a God who would send her there because she had chosen to reject Him. She had a choice. She could choose Jesus or not. I believe in a God who was kind enough to give her a choice. Our conversation that day did not answer every question, but it removed an offense between her and God.

Months would go by before she brought up any conversation about God, Christians, or homosexuality. In the meantime, I seemed to have a little more favor with her, and her guardedness toward me was suddenly gone.

***

"Drew, why do Christians hate gay people?"

Her question hit during the lull between the morning rush and the lunch rush as I was making mocha mix. When I turned to look at her, I saw no anger or hostility, just a subtle, vulnerable pain.

"Do you feel like I hate you?" I asked, both out of sincere curiosity and hope that I had demonstrated compassion through our interactions.

"Well, no...but other Christians. Why do they hate gay people?"

I answered cautiously, "Christian's don't hate gay people."

"Yes they do! I have seen them at the Portland Pride Parade with their signs. They are so hateful! They have screamed at me and insulted me. And I see them on the news always picketing gay events. They are incredibly hateful to us!"

My heart broke. I knew what she was talking about, and I knew she had a point. I thought, "Here goes." Aloud, I said, "Well, first let me say that I am sorry for the way you have been treated by people who claim the name of Jesus. You are right. There are people in the Church who act horribly to the gay community. But I want you to know that there are also many of us in the Church who feel that such people are *not* reflecting the heart of God. Again, I am so sorry for how you have been treated. I am sorry for how Christ has been represented to you."

She said nothing, and for a few moments, we silently went about our tasks.

Then she asked, "So...if how those people have treated us is not 'God's heart'..." she used air quotes here, "... then what's the big problem? Why can't you all just accept us, and...I don't know, bless us?"

This was a weighty question. Unlike the "Am I going to hell?" question months earlier, this one was not loaded with anger or hostility. It came from a place of hurt over the rejection she had felt for years. However, like the hell question, answering this one was going to be delicate. Once again, asking the Holy Spirit to give me wisdom, I ventured into the minefield.

"Well, one of the reasons is a fundamental disconnect between how you understand your identity and how we understand your identity."

She looked puzzled. "What do you mean?"

"You are sexually attracted to women, and you engage in sexual behavior with women, and those two things inform your identity. You feel like a lesbian, you act like a lesbian, you are a lesbian. Does that sound fair?"

She furrowed her brow, "Seems a bit simplistic..."

"I know. It's more complex than that, but for the sake of the question, would you agree that your identity as a lesbian is, on a baseline level, informed by your feelings and behavior?"

She relaxed a bit, "Yeah, that makes sense."

I continued, "One of the major problems for Christians, then, is that we view those attractions as temptations toward sin, and we view the behavior as a sinful behavior that the Bible has commanded people not to engage in. So, essentially, what I hear you asking of me, as a Christian, is to affirm and even celebrate an identity that is based in temptation and sinful behavior. That is something I can't do."

She stood there, trying to absorb what I had just said. I could tell there was still a disconnect. It is the same disconnect on both sides of the issue that gets triggered when Christians, who mean well but just sound mean, say, "love the sinner, hate the sin" in reference to the LGBTQ community. Christians don't understand that when they say that, they might as well be saying to that community, "I hate you!" because their identities are almost inseparably bound to their feelings and behavior. To the LGBTQ person, rejecting the behavior is rejecting the person.

As we awkwardly and silently went about our work, I had an idea. "Let me put it another way. This weekend is Portland Pride, right?"

She squinted slightly, and cautiously responded "Yeah, why?"

"Go with me on this for another minute. The Bible calls adultery a sin. Can you imagine the conflict I, as a Christian, might have if there was a celebration and a parade for adulterers? And then if I was asked to celebrate and affirm the participants of that parade in their identity as adulterers?"

She quickly shot back, "Being gay and committing adultery is not the same thing!"

"I agree with you." I took a deep breath and said, "but according to the Bible, both behaviors are sin. I understand that there are all sorts of issues we are not addressing right now, but let me focus on what is the same for a second. I could no sooner affirm or celebrate an identity based in the act of adultery than I could affirm or bless an identity based in homosexual feelings or behavior. That is not how I see you."

She was becoming visibly frustrated and somewhat defensive, and I completely understood why. I was challenging her understanding of her identity, and every single one of us would begin to get defensive in the same situation.

She leveled a look at me. "OK. So then how do you see me?"

Silently, I prayed, "Oh, please let me get this right, Lord!"

Aloud, I said, "I see you as a woman who was created in the image of God. You are a woman loved by a God who gave His Son so that He could be in relationship with you. I see you as a woman God gave a free will to, so you have all the freedom in the world to make your own choices about what to believe and how to live—even if those choices go against what God would desire for you. I see you as valuable and worthy of every bit of respect, dignity, and kindness that I would extend to anyone else—and that I would hope to have extended to me. I see you as kind, funny, hardworking, compassionate, and feisty. And although I do not agree with—nor am able to affirm or celebrate your accepted sexual identity—I respect and accept that you have the right to understand yourself how you choose."

Silence.

This conversation was emotionally charged for both of us. I wondered what she was thinking. Was she offended? Did she hear my heart? Did she understand what I was trying to communicate?

Finally, a sound broke the silence. "Huh."

That was it. The sum of her response to this interaction. Then the lunch hour rush started, and it would be several weeks before we would touch on these topics again.

***

"So...Drew. My partner and I have been reading some books together, and we are feeling really nervous."

"What book are you all reading that has you worried?"

I truly did not see this one coming.

"Well," she replied, "it is actually a series of books. Have you heard of *Left Behind*?"

When she named that infamous title, a thousand thoughts went shooting through my head. For your entertainment, here are just a few: "Where did they get *those* books? How many have they read? I'd rather they were reading a Bible, but I'll work with what I've got! She isn't going to ask me about the antichrist, is she?! *Oh, sweet Lord, I hope she hasn't found the movie!*" And the last thought that went through my mind must have been the Holy Spirit speaking because all He said was: "Drew! Your face...fix your face!"

I stammered, "Uhh... *Left Behind?* Sure. You say you are concerned?" I was trying to reign in my thoughts.

"Well, yeah!" she responded emphatically. "Are we really going to be left behind like that if we don't know Jesus?"

I thought about how to answer this. "Well, people in the Church have different interpretations about what the world will look like before Jesus returns. *Left Behind* is a story based on one interpretation of how it will play out. Do you remember our conversation months ago, when I said that if you are not reconciled to God the Father through Jesus, *that* is the reason people end up in hell?"

Wide-eyed and nervous she said, "Yes...well, my girlfriend and I have been thinking that maybe we need to find a church and start going."

I couldn't believe what I was hearing. Trying to keep my face in order, I said, "Well, yeah. That would be a really good step to getting to know Jesus."

"Yeah," she said. "We found some churches online that are 'welcoming and embracing' to the gay community. We think we might start with one of those churches. What do you think about that?"

I could tell by her tone that she was experiencing a conflict with what she was suggesting. I thought a moment. "Can you tell me what you mean by 'welcoming and embracing'?"

She answered, "They don't believe homosexual acts are sin. There are even a few churches with gay pastors. Wouldn't it be OK to go to one of those?"

The last thing that I wanted to do was to crush what clearly was a move of the Holy Spirit to draw her to the Lord. But I knew, once again, that I was going to have to say some things that were going to be difficult for her to hear. That was the risk. But I had to be faithful to the truth.

I took a deep breath and went for it. "Here is what you have to consider, and trust me when I say that I understand the difficulty of what I am about to say to you. The Bible is full of difficult teachings. It challenges us in our relationship with Jesus to lay our lives fully down to His authority. It goes against our own sense of self-preservation and entitlement. It calls us to die to our own desires and to allow the Spirit of God to transform us. Many people have said that when the Bible says no to homosexual behavior, it is only addressing specific types and, therefore, can be ignored, but the *only* sexual union the Bible affirms is sex between a man and woman in the covenant of marriage. I believe that any time someone claims the Bible is OK with homosexual behavior, they are trying to get around a teaching that is, admittedly, difficult for them to swallow. I understand the temptation to interpret Scripture in a way that allows for this, but doing so shifts away from truth. Bottom line: The Bible never affirms any sex outside of that within marriage between a man and woman. If a church tells you differently, how can you trust that they are not also shifting and changing other important but difficult teachings in the Scriptures?"

She nodded her head. Apparently, the Holy Spirit was already saying the same thing to her. What she said next broke my heart. "But if I go somewhere where they teach the truth, I am afraid they will reject me."

Fortunately, I knew of a few churches that were faithful to teach the truth but would also be safe places for my coworker and her girlfriend to learn more about Jesus without fearing that they would be rejected. I gave her a list of churches and encouraged her to take the risk.

And then back to making mochas, lattes, and espressos we went.

A few weeks later, my coworker quit the coffee shop, and I never saw her again. I would like to say she gave her life over to Jesus, but I don't know where her story went. All I know is that in the brief season of our friendship, I was able to remove some obstacles between her and Jesus. I was able to tell her the truth in love and point her in the direction of a God who loved her and wanted relationship with her. I was able to give her a different experience of interacting with people who claim to believe in Jesus.

The end result of our interactions is not my responsibility. That is between her and the Lord. But I did my part by speaking the truth I felt the Lord wanted her to hear and treating her with love and grace.

Chapter 7

Changed

OK. Full disclosure. Do you know what question I have hated more than any other question over the last twenty years of my personal journey? Here it is: "Have you really changed?"

Oh, the expectations and demands behind that question. I mean, what objective qualifiers can you use to say that I have changed? What measuring stick? Not to be crass, but exactly how "un-gay" do I need to be to be able to prove that I've changed?

On top of all that, I have to deal with another judgement folks toss out: that I was never "really gay" to begin with! Well, again, not to be crass, but I felt pretty gay when I was engaging in sexual behavior with my boyfriend. What else can I say?

Here is a quick analogy. Let's say you've been overweight for a long period of time. Maybe you eat horribly. Maybe the fast food drive-in window attendants all know you by name. Maybe your idea of exercise is actually walking *in* to the fast-food restaurant. Point being, if you're not healthy, you are probably cultivating an unhealthy lifestyle. Maybe the reason you're unhealthy is that you don't know what to do to get healthy or you don't even believe you have the power to change your current state of health.

Now, let's say that on your journey to get in shape, you decide to change just one aspect of your life. Say you start to eat healthy. That act is a good move in the right direction. You may start to feel better. You may begin to lose weight. That is positive change. But just changing one act of health is not going to completely transform you. Sure, you might lose a few inches, but those inches will remain flabby. Total transformation requires a holistic approach. It's going take more than just diet to transform you into a vibrantly healthy being; it's going to take diet, exercise, drinking more water, and getting more sleep. And such transformation will not happen without consistency and longevity.

But say you are just in the first stages of this health journey. You began eating well, and you are exercising. How do you feel? I can tell you, and I will in a minute. I can tell you because this analogy is a present reality for me. I am currently a bit fat. Well, maybe that's a little too harsh. Maybe for the sake of personal kindness, I'll just say I am squishy around the edges. Since I became a speaker who travels around the country, I've been eating too often in hotel rooms and airports, and I have gained "a bit" of weight. Well, honestly, it's more like I gained a toddler.

Recently, I began taking steps to correct that. I wanted to stop feeling ashamed when I see pictures of myself. That's my shallow reason. My more noble reason is that I want to be a healthier dad and husband. So, I have begun to exercise. As I write this, it's been about a month into this journey, and I already feel positive changes. I'm not an Adonis yet. I am nowhere near the personal confidence required to jog through the streets without a shirt on—thank goodness, that's not my goal. I mean, come on, nobody wants to see that foolishness right now. But I can already tell my body is making subtle changes. It's really exciting, encouraging, and gratifying.

Here's the secondary reality of this season. I freaking *hurt*. The other day, I did a few too many leg exercises. To say I was sore the next day would be one of the greatest understatements ever uttered by all of mankind. I felt sorry for my wife and kids. The moaning and groaning I made every time I got up from the couch was comical or annoying—take your pick. And then I had to use the bathroom....

Yes friends, I fell onto the toilet when my quads and hamstrings gave out underneath me. And there I sat for quite some time. Not quite able to get up. Trying to devise a plan that would not require me calling my wife for help. I don't know if our love life would have survived that moment.

Oh the joys of transformation!

If I had evaluated the merit of the transformation I was experiencing based on that one moment—and how I felt about the moment—I probably would have stopped my journey right then and there. In that moment, I did not feel stronger. I did not feel transformed into what I wanted to be. I did not feel healthier. I felt pathetic and weak. And I can tell you this; the humiliation didn't stop there. In the first month of working out, I think my tally of times vomiting at the gym was up to eight. Those are not my proudest moments.

In past seasons of immaturity, I would have probably decided that such pain meant I was on the wrong track—that this pursuit was not worth the humiliation, pain, or effort. As understandable as that conclusion might be, I can tell you from experience in other areas of my life that such an interpretation is extremely shortsighted. The soreness and muscle weakness are part of the process of transformation. When you lift weights, your muscles are actually being torn. After this micro-tearing, the body then repairs the muscles to make them stronger. Tear down, build up.

My trainer assures me I won't feel this sore and weak forever. It's true for my body, and it's true emotionally and spiritually. Transformation is happening. Under the surface, maybe, but it's happening. And soon I will begin to see the visible evidence of it. That makes all the pain and humiliation worth it.

Transformation is not a light switch; it's more like the sunrise. Let me tell you a little story. When I was twenty-one, I worked at the front desk of an athletic club (trust me, I get the irony). That was the last time in my life that I was relatively in shape. That was also the time right after I had begun being honest with myself and my church community about my struggle with same-sex attraction.

I desired to be faithful to the Lord and walk in obedience to his Word, but in light of my struggle and history, I was feeling very overwhelmed. Nothing I had in my "transformation arsenal" was changing my attractions in a way I could see. I kept praying and memorizing Scripture, but my attractions felt like they were never going to go away. In fact, I had no guarantee they ever *would* go away. At that point, I had never heard a testimony of someone who had overcome this type of struggle. I felt completely alone and stuck.

I worked the opening shift every morning. In order to get everything ready for the club members, I had to be there at 4 AM. That was fine with me. I'm generally a morning person, and at that time in my life, I didn't mind the solitude of those mornings, even though I'm an extrovert. Bonus: When the place was empty, I could loudly and aggressively pray out my frustrations with the Lord. If you had been a fly on the wall near the pool every morning when I removed its cover, I can guarantee you would've heard some spirited prayers coming out of my mouth. And by spirited, I don't mean Holy-Spirit-inspired prayers; these sounded more like a foul-mouthed sailor had just stubbed his toe on the bedframe. (For the record, I still believe those are the most authentic, effective prayers. But I digress.)

One of my favorite things about that job was the view from the front desk, which faced an eastern wall of floor-to-ceiling windows. I could watch the sun rise every morning.

I had plenty of quiet time between when the first group of members came in around 5 AM and when the second, larger, group came around 6:30. I could sit, ponder, and pray.

There is something about being consistently awake before the rest of humanity. It forces silence. Each morning, when I rose and got ready for work, I did so quietly because my roommates were still asleep. When I drove to work, I did not turn on my stereo—that just seemed rude before 4 AM. When I arrived at work, the building was empty and quiet. I knew I would not see another soul for at least an hour. And even when club members began to arrive, 5 AM is just not a chatty time. Consequently, for a good year of my life, I spent almost the first almost two hours of my day, five days a week, in relative silence.

As my friends and family can tell you, I generally don't choose to be alone; I like to be with people. So that season could have either been a special brand of torture or incredibly intentional. Thankfully, the Lord helped me make it intentional.

And so, every morning, during that lull between rushes, at that front desk, I would watch the sun slowly rise. Sometimes I listened to God. Sometimes I read: the Bible, C. S. Lewis's *Mere Christianity,* and other books to enrich my faith. Sometimes I prayed. As I said, most of my prayers were spirited ones. Forced silence has a way of bringing to the surface things your heart wants to ignore. Alone at the front desk of that athletic club, I uttered things in brutal honesty to God that I never would have confessed in my church sanctuary.

I should mention that I have always struggled with some level of insecurity. One particular insecurity has been my masculinity. My given name is Andrew, which means "strong and manly." For years I viewed my name as either profoundly ironic or a cruel, cosmic joke. And then I ended up working the front desk of an athletic club, watching a parade of near-perfect physical specimens of masculinity walk in the door every day. The disparity between the masculinity I perceived in them and the utter lack I perceived in myself assaulted my heart.

I made some deep and painful confessions and accusations to God. I questioned why He'd made me a man. I confessed lusting after what I saw. These were no pretty dialogues with the Lord, but they were very sanctifying for me over the long haul.

One of these mornings, as I was feeling angry that the Lord didn't seem to be doing anything about my pain, I heard Him tenderly speak to me. It went something like this:

"Drew, did you notice that the sun is up?"

This took me off guard, because I was feeling even more angry, hurt, and insecure than usual. This question seemed way off topic. "Yes, I did. So what!?" (I was so teachable back then.)

The Lord replied, "When you got to work today, it was pitch black outside."

I started to get annoyed. "Again, so what? That's how it is every day. What's your point?"

The Lord patiently and gently replied, "When did it change from dark to light?"

As I sat and thought about His question, I began to realize the beautiful—and yet unwanted—answer; there was no single, distinct moment when the sky went from dark to light. The change was incremental and subtle.

I sat with this question, in silence, over the coming days. Every morning as the sun came up, I would get ready to watch and study it. I thought if I could catch the moment the sun peeked over the hills, I'd see it. But over the next few mornings, just as that sunrise was about to happen, a club member would walk in, I would turn to greet them, and when I turned back, the sun would be up. Or another distraction would hit, and I would be facing the wall across from the windows, and all of a sudden, I'd notice the sunlight hitting the wall. By the time I'd spin around, the sun would be up. It became comical how I missed the moment every morning— for days.

And then, one morning I finally caught the sun coming over the horizon. It was one of the most anticipated sunrises of my life, and it was glorious. The sky glowed pink, orange, and indigo. Yet in the beauty of the moment, I realized that even though the sun had broken through the horizon, light had been slowly overcoming the darkness long before the breakthrough occurred. That was the Lord's answer to me. There *would* be a day when the sun cleared the horizon, and it would be beautiful and glorious—but even long before that moment, the Lord would be actively displacing the dark with the light.

When it came to insecurity about my masculinity, that is exactly how the Lord has worked healing in me. I was in a dark place for a while. My identity had been distorted, and I had not viewed myself as qualified to be a man. But I began and continued to heal.

Healing can be a slow and incremental process as God illuminates His goodness and intentionality. He has done this for me in a multitude of ways, both obvious and subtle. And as I have grown more and more secure over the years, He has poured more light on me and on His purpose for me as a man. There have been many beautiful moments, but there wasn't a single specific moment where it shifted from dark to light. In fact, He is still pouring light in to shadowed places.

How is He accomplishing this?

I have believed wrong things about manhood and masculinity. Actually, I think we all have. But the thing is, we don't know what we don't know. Call it deception or call it blind spots. Maybe it is just timing or maturity. Whatever you call it, we all believe falsehoods, and we all hold ourselves to standards that either have nothing to do with reality or are distortions of reality. These can quickly become strongholds of condemnation that rob us of joy and peace as they cripple our lives. Sadly, we usually have no idea these strongholds are operating in our lives until the Lord sheds light on them.

That is what the Lord did for me, starting with those mornings at the front desk. Every day, I faced the images of masculinity that I felt I lacked. Facing what I believed I could never attain exposed in my heart what I coveted in others and what I despised in myself. It was painful and embarrassing but necessary. It made me admit and articulate what I thought masculinity was, and what it wasn't. It made me confess and declare what I believed to be true about other men and what I believed to be true about myself. It revealed merciless and marginalizing standards. When all that ugly was exposed, the Lord then spent several years confronting, deconstructing, and rebuilding what I believed to be masculinity. He helped me to see it in other men and affirm it in them, and He helped me see it in myself.

He is *still* doing this. I am not done yet, but I can tell you that I shifted from crippling insecurity to security in believing I belong in the world of men. It happened, but it is also still happening. He continues to help me grow in my understanding of myself as a good man.

So back to my current journey: the one to transform my physical body from something resembling jello to something less jiggly. The other day, I took a class at the gym that pushed the limits of my physical ability. At some point, an unaddressed wound in my life rose up. A rush of old condemnation began surging over my spirit and mind with an incredible amount of force. I left the class—which, by the way, was hard for everyone that morning—and headed for the bathroom. As I closed the door, I broke down crying.

Yep: a grown man in tears at the gym bathroom because he felt like a failure. It was something deep in the recesses of my heart and history that I hadn't touched because I had never been in the context to touch it. All my self-condemnation and self-hatred in the realm of exercise and weight rooms—birthed out of painful and traumatic experiences I did not choose—heaved to the surface.

When I finally left the bathroom, the other members of my gym—all friends—were ready and waiting to encourage me and confront the lies and criticisms I was buried under. (By the way, I have the best community on earth.)

God continues to shine His light into the shadows of my heart. There is not a single light-switch moment. It is an ever-increasing, incremental process. Further in, Further up.

Why share this story?

Over my last year of teaching engagements, one of the more common concerns audiences bring up is how to respond to gender-identity issues. This is a growing concern among believers, and it is a topic that deserves serious and thoughtful attention. But I am concerned about the continued focus on what to do about "them out there" while we forget to pull the metaphorical log out of our own eyes.

In the Church, we often get focused on what we see as problems with the world, and we forget to question whether we are engaging issues from a healthy, helpful, or spiritually accurate place. I believe that as the Church seeks to effectively minister to gender-identity issues—or rather, masculinity and femininity—we need to honestly evaluate our approach. Are we starting from a biblically informed view of gender or from a culturally informed view?

I have known and ministered to too many men and women—some from a same-sex attraction background, some not—who have felt like failures in their gender because they felt they didn't measure up to a certain standard, didn't display the "right" character traits, interests, body type, or temperament. But those standards were strictly cultural—

none of them were based in a biblical revelation of masculinity or femininity.

I have no doubt that God has created male and female as distinctly different, and we can rely on His Word to discern many of those distinctions. I also have no doubt that if we believe God intentionally creates us in His image—as male *and* female—than we can also rightly believe what God's Word affirms: that He purposefully designs us individually in the womb, fearfully and wonderfully.

So, if he made me a man, and He made me unique, then He has a unique plan for me as a man. He made you on purpose and for a purpose, too.

Even though I now confidently know that God intended me to be a man, I encounter a bit of a problem; He also intended me to be artistic, intuitive, sensitive, and dramatic. These are all traits that, if I view masculinity strictly through the distorted values of my culture, are deemed feminine. They are the traits I hated and despised in myself, and so it was more difficult for me to see my manhood as a blessing. But as God has continually been illuminating His heart and intentions for me, as I've stepped into my vocation as a public speaker, pastoral counselor, and father to three daughters, I see the goodness of His intentional design. I see how these traits can be places that my masculinity flows out of, not hindrances or barriers to masculinity itself.

Obviously, there is much more to this conversation than my own ideas. Many books and resources have helped me as I have wrestled through these issues. One book I highly recommend to help navigate this discussion is *Fully Alive: A Biblical Vision of Gender That Frees Men and Women to Live Beyond Stereotypes*, by Dr. Larry Crabb. This book deconstructs cultural masculinity and femininity and looks at these two distinctions through the image of God.

I'd also like to suggest that we, as believers, submit our ideas about masculinity and femininity to the Lord and allow Him to challenge and remove all that is unworthy of His image. I think that would be powerfully redemptive for so many of us.

***

There's another aspect of change and transformation that we need to talk about: reverting. What happens when people who were presumably following Jesus—and seemed to experience transformation—suddenly revert to places of brokenness? This is one of the greatest frustrations in my particular area of ministry.

This issue also hits many of us in other areas of faith: our understanding of salvation, eternal security, the power of God to change particular issues, whether or not transformation is real—the whole shebang. Really, this is a doozy of an issue.

In March 2001, I travelled to New York City with my friend and former boss, Jason Thompson, of Portland Fellowship. We were to be guests on the Sally Jesse Raphael show in an episode titled, "Gay to Straight?"

No, I don't recommend you Google this show, even though it is still somewhere on YouTube. They filmed us for about a half an hour, but they edited us to look like complete idiots in the few-minute-segment that actually aired. It was not a great representation of our stories or ministry. In retrospect, one of the most frustrating aspects of that experience was the episode's title.

In fact, I'd like to take a minute here to explain something. For a number of years, I was a part of what some have called the ex-gay movement. Our ministry, Portland Fellowship, was under the umbrella of a ministry called Exodus International. One of the ways they branded their message, and Portland Fellowship as well, was with the tagline: "Change is possible." Yes, you could interpret that as saying people go from gay to straight. But remember what I said about change and transformation; it is not a light switch. It is more like the sunrise. It is gradual. It is a process, and it continues.

Change is a fluid continuum. How you move along it depends on what you're investing into your heart, spirit, and body. So, when the show presented a change of sexual identity as a switch from gay to straight, it set up a false dilemma. If you simply switch over, there's not a lot of room for process or the understanding of transformation. It is black and white, pass or fail.

At the time that show was filmed, I was not nearly as addicted to the things I had been before. My identity had shifted. I had more hope than I ever had in my entire life, and I was relating to people in a far healthier way than I had been before.

And as for my attractions, the severity, intensity, and frequency were all vastly changing. But they weren't gone. I was not instantly transformed into a raging heterosexual with overwhelming desires for boobies and whatnot. Pardon the crassness, but it seemed like the premise of the show almost required that type of transformation for me to be legit and not be labeled a self-hating, self-deceived gay.

Granted, I was not exactly where I wanted to be yet, but I was certainly not where I'd been before.

Here's the problem, and it remains a problem even today when people ask me, "Have you really changed?" The expectation of change in sexual identification is sometimes tyrannical. Unless someone completely eradicates every shred of desire, temptation, and memory, forever and ever amen, then their journey of transformation is considered invalid. Somehow, they are a liar and fraud, and they are leading people to destruction. I'm not exaggerating here—people have said these exact things to me and worse.

Back to the analogy about physical fitness transformation. Say you were sixty pounds overweight. You began diligently eating better, working out, getting more sleep, and drinking more water. Eventually, you lose twenty pounds, and you are well on your way to your goal. You will look different, and you will feel different. Your behaviors are different, and your attitude is probably going to be different. You are transforming. No one is going to say you're a failure because you have not immediately and completely lost all sixty pounds. Quite the opposite: They will encourage you and tell you you're doing so well—keep it up!

That's generally what people do when they see change; they encourage people on their trajectory, because they see the evidence. And once you do reach that sixty-pound weight-loss goal and you are in the shape you want to be, no one will suggest that you stop exercising and eating well. In fact, we instinctively know that in order to maintain a particular state of health and transformation, we have to continue with the behaviors that got us there. Those healthy behaviors, attitudes, and patterns create the transformation.

I love watching weight-loss programs on TV. I always root for the contestants. Each one of them who steps on the scale during the finale to reveal their weight loss—whether it is 150 pounds or 200 pounds—has experienced a real transformation. We all see the tangible evidence of it.

Unfortunately, we also often see the evidence that those very same people—after experiencing a life-changing transformation—end up transforming right back into what they were to begin with. To maintain the transformation, you have to keep doing the things that transformed you in the first place.

We could debate the healthiness of the speed of transformation demonstrated on those programs. If your transformation process isn't sustainable long-term, it's not gonna be successful long-term. And if you are driven by unrealistic expectations, then inevitably you are going to grow weary under the weight of them.

But here's the thing: Often, the contestants on the weight-loss programs are under incredible amounts of pressure to transform radically and dramatically in a very short period of time. Which means that the pace of the transformation process is extremely demanding and usually unsustainable for normal life. On many of these programs, people go away to a ranch for months on end, leaving their normal life behind without any of the responsibilities or trappings of daily life. They focus only on weight loss and transformation. That does not prepare them to return to real life and maintain that transformation.

We are not a patient culture. We live in the instant-download generation. If you've been around more than a few decades, you've witnessed an exponential shift in conveniences. Remember dial-up Internet service? No? Well here's how it went. When you wanted to use the Internet, you would sign on and hear the shrill sound of the modem connecting. You'd watch a page load, sometimes lines of pixels at a time. But you were excited over this marvel of invention! The Internet! You were fine with waiting patiently, maybe even going and getting a snack while your email loaded because it was still revolutionary to receive electronic mail—you didn't have to wait for a letter to cross the country in a truck! Your letter arrived instantly (or, rather, after a minute or so). Today, if that email does not appear on my screen the second I click it, I'm ready to change servers!

Remember, I grew up with VHS. In order to rent a video, you had to drive to the video store. You had to look through the shelves to find the video. If the person who last rented the video hadn't done the "be kind and rewind" thing, you'd have to rewind the sucker when you got it back home. All this before you could even start your movie. And if you wanted to skip forward or backward in the video, that was a process as well. Now we have video on demand. And so help me God, if that little download bar or spinny wheel does not hurry up and load my VOD, then my whole evening is inconvenienced.

The point of this little tirade is: We are neither patient nor long-suffering. Our culture has surrendered to the god of convenience. If our culture had an idol that we bowed down to, it would be the great, golden calf named instant gratification. Transformation is *not* instant, it is *not* convenient, and the process is often less than gratifying.

To rant—I mean, repeat: A journey out of sexual brokenness is *not* like flicking on a light switch. It is not a destination you get to without having to do anything further.

Many people who once claimed transformation in the area of their sexual identities and attractions reversed their course and now proclaim a message to the contrary. I know many such individuals personally, and I grieve over their life choices. Don't get me wrong: I understand their circumstances, and I understand how they got where they are. I understand the difficulty of living in transformation. It's not a passive pursuit, and it's never done.

It's dangerous to begin flirting with things you know in your heart are not right, healthy, good, or permitted scripturally—especially if you've done so before and know your own vulnerabilities with those things. This is not rocket science; it's Scripture. If you sow to please the flesh, from the flesh you will reap destruction. But if you sow to please the Spirit, from the Spirit you reap life. And we never stop needing to sow.

When people ask me, "Have you changed?" they are usually thinking of the long list of people who once claimed to have changed but who now are right back where they started. I understand why people ask. The doubt behind the questioning is really on us as Christians; if we communicate that transformation is like switching a light switch, verses how the Scripture describes sanctification and transformation, then we can't criticize the world when they question our transformation.

The "have you changed?" question bothers me most when it comes from people who profess faith in Christ. Why? I think because the words *changed* and *cured* have become synonymous in this context. That is a very distorted view of Christian spiritual formation and discipleship. It completely leaves out process. It sets up a pass/fail evaluation if you do experience residual moments of vulnerability or temptation or if you fall into sinful behavior once in a while. It creates an inability to be honest about the process of transformation. But I think the other thing that drives me crazy about the question is its origin of skepticism. On one level, people question the validity of whether I personally have experienced change, but on a deeper level, they are questioning whether Jesus can transform sexual brokenness.

Let me ask you; when did our sexual desires become more powerful then Almighty God? I mean, really! If you believe in the God who created the universe; who brings our spirits from death to life; who conquers sin, death, and the devil; who created you and is giving you the breath in your lungs right now—if you believe in that God, do you really think sexuality is the one thing too big for Him?

Now some people say God doesn't need us to change our sexual desires because He created us with them. They say He doesn't need to change our sexuality because He blesses same-sex attraction. (I fully disagree with both of those arguments, but that's another discussion for another time.) If you believe God shouldn't have to or doesn't need to transform sexual desires because He blesses them, it still begs the question: *Can* He transform your sexuality? Is He powerful enough to do that?

Part of the beauty of God's power at work in us is that He partners with our decisions. He doesn't force good choices, and He doesn't force healing. He doesn't force anything on us. It's our choice completely how we engage with Him and how we access His power. It's our choice if we choose to deny His power and live in weakness or separation from Him. He does not force our hand. And yes, it is possible to live a disconnected, disobedient, neutered "Christian" life. Scripture speaks to this type of "faith": "holding to a form of [outward] godliness (religion), although they have denied its power [for their conduct nullifies their claim of faith]..." (2 Tim. 3:5 AMP).

So, what do I think when I am asked, "Have you changed?" I am frustrated, but I am also joyful that I can fully and completely proclaim that God has proved powerful in my life. He has and is still transforming my heart in so many ways that it would take volumes of books to lay it all out. For brevity, I will say this: He's changed my identity far beyond my past perception of myself as a sexual struggler or as a broken individual. I now know I am His son, and I am loved, and I am accepted.

He has also given me the privilege of being known as the husband to my wife and the father to my children. Those are two identities I once thought were impossible for me. And He's even given me the opportunity to be known as a pastor. It is a wonderful privilege to be able to shepherd people's hearts toward Jesus. In every aspect of my life, God continues to transform me into greater Christlikeness.

He has also changed my desires. Yes, once upon a time I desired illicit sex with men, and I even fulfilled that desire. But today, I can say with full confidence that I desire only sexual relationship with my wife. And that's an interesting thing, too. I used to think transformation would look like having the same feelings I was having for men, except that they would be directed at the opposite sex. That mindset is actually pretty broken. That would have been trading one struggle with lust and brokenness for another struggle with lust and brokenness—just with a different sex target. No, God did not want to trade lust for lust, but rather brokenness for wholeness. And from the overflow of wholeness, I have the responsibility to steward my sexuality in a healthy way.

I am not saying I could never again be vulnerable to moving backward or cultivating lust in my life. When you move from a pass/fail, on/off, gay-to-straight view of transformation to viewing transformation as a journey or process, you have to acknowledge the need for continued stewardship and the potential of digression or failure. I can't claim that it is impossible for me to have a random attraction or for a memory to surface that could tempt me to cultivate lust or a homosexual thought. Jesus erased my guilt, shame, and condemnation—not my history or memory or humanity. The reality is that I am a human being, and I have vulnerabilities; we all do. I can either cultivate my vulnerabilities and temptations, or I can cultivate holiness and health and righteousness.

In my past, even an un-acted-upon temptation would have done me in for months. These days, if I have a difficult day, or hour, or even a moment when I recognize something coming after my heart, I have the opportunity and freedom to bring those things to Jesus, submit them to Him, and walk in the freedom He died to give me.

This is hard to hear if you think of change like the light switch—and completely without any vulnerability or possibility to fail. I know my answers may not be satisfactory to you, but they're honest and realistic, and I am able to live a very full and wonderful life within the reality of them. Freedom and transformation do not require the absence of temptation or vulnerability. The absence of struggle does not determine success. The reality is: I am no longer obligated to those temptations. I have the free and wonderful choice to walk in the direction that Christ has called me, and I am full of joy and satisfaction on that walk.

My heart often returns to a statement I heard on my very first night at the discipleship program at Portland Fellowship. The ministry director at the time, Phil Hobizal, spoke some powerful and freeing words to our group—words we often repeated when a new person came to our ministry. He said: "Portland Fellowship is not here to turn you straight. We don't have the power to do that. But what we *are* here to do is to draw you into deeper relationship with Jesus, and *He* will transform you. *He* will tell you who you are. Because the opposite of homosexuality is not heterosexuality; it's holiness."

Chapter 8

An (Un)common Love Story

I want to make a disclosure; this is a vulnerable chapter for me to write. Not because I'm going to disclose any deep sinful information. Not because I'm going to expose any wounds from my childhood. And not because of anything shameful. In fact, this chapter is about one of the best things in my life. The reason that writing it is vulnerable for me is because of the inevitable and unfortunate level of skepticism that I experience when I share this part of my story.

This chapter is about how I met and fell in love with my wife.

Now, for the average guy, saying that would be perfectly normal. I mean, there's even a popular television series called *How I Met Your Mother*. Generally, a love story is engaging—and it's taken on its own merit. But as someone who walked out of homosexual attraction and activity, I don't get the luxury of simply telling the story of how I met Suzanne. I have to emotionally and mentally brace myself for the incredulous looks, or invasive questions, or general level of disbelief that I deal with. I often feel I have to defend something that most people take for granted. And that's tender for me.

The other reason this is not easy is because I have felt the pressure to feel somewhat apologetic for this aspect of my testimony. It's the strangest thing. In my years of ministry, helping men and women walk out of homosexuality, a weird feeling would sometimes creep in. I found myself wanting to apologize for being married. I don't know how to explain it, except to say that because of the skepticism toward transformation in the struggle of homosexuality, it was like I had to apologize for the reality that my life *had* changed. I think people assumed I was trying to prove I had changed by marrying a woman and that I was diminishing other people in their journey because they hadn't gotten to that point. Oh, and any reluctance on my part to disclose the intimate details of our sexual life and connection immediately put my marriage under scrutiny. Can you imagine requiring such disclosures from any other acquaintances as proof that their marriage was valid? This might sound ridiculous from the outside, but I assure you it's a real thing.

Don't get me wrong. I understand that because of the nature of my story and ministry, these assumptions are just the nature of the beast. I am not complaining or whining, just bracing myself.

Sooooo....without any further ado or fuss, let's get to the story.

About three years into my process of surrendering my broken sexuality to Christ, I begin to wonder whether marriage to a woman was possible for me. I still had some temptations and struggles with same-sex attraction. Granted, they were not nearly as prominent or pervasive as they had been, but I was still dealing with occasional falls into pornography and fantasy. There were also the lingering memories of my past sexual involvement. These realities made me wonder if I would ever reach a place where I would be healed enough to walk into a relationship with a woman. I mean, did I even want that? Girls were scary!

I had always appreciated the beauty of women. I had no problem recognizing and even being drawn to the beauty and grace I saw in women, and I was beginning to appreciate the differences between men and women. A better way to put it: I was beginning to affirm my own masculinity. I was finally beginning to appreciate that I actually *did* belong in the world of men.

At this point in my history, I wouldn't say I recognized a strong or even noticeable sexual attraction to women. In fact, I would say one of the greatest obstacles I needed to overcome was understanding the difference between lust and love and how those two translate into attraction.

This can be a huge challenge for people emerging from sexual brokenness. We might think we need to put off forming a healthy romantic relationship until we feel the same or similar feelings to the lust we were once controlled by. After all, shouldn't romantic love be erotic? Shouldn't it be powerful?

Well, yes. It should be all those things. But lust and love are very, very different animals. If I was waiting to feel for a woman what I had once felt for men, I would be trying to recreate an unhealthy attraction sourced in lust. My attraction to men and my involvement with homosexual behavior were driven greatly by unmet need, defilement, and lust. These attractions and behaviors were inherently very selfish and self-serving and were *not* going to make a healthy foundation for a marriage.

We can apply that reality to heterosexual relationships as well. If you're walking into marriage and the basis of your relationship is lust, unmet needs, and/or defilement, you are not going to have a good marriage. No person of either gender can meet all your needs or restore your brokenness. You might disagree with what I'm going to say next, but I'll say it anyway. I believe homosexual attraction—just like many manifestations of sexual brokenness—is a product of brokenness, and forming a relationship based on the attempt to fix something that's broken rather than simply loving from the overflow of the heart is not the basis for a healthy relationship.

Therefore, if I was waiting to be attracted to a woman in the way I had been attracted to a man, I had the wrong goal.

And once I understood that, yet another obstacle arose: the contrast between healthy sexual attraction and lust. I knew I didn't want to feel the same thing I used to feel for guys, but what was I supposed to feel? What example could I look to understand *healthy* sexuality in marriage?

I hope we all can agree that lust is not a good basis for marriage. Lust is intrinsically selfish, and anyone who's been married for more than five minutes knows that the surest deathblow to a healthy marriage is selfishness. But I saw so many marriages that were defined by a selfish need to be completed by one's spouse. I do believe God purposes marriage as a sacrament to display a complete picture of His image; in that sense, it is about being made whole. But that kind of divine completion is a far cry from saying to another flawed human being: "I need you to make me feel whole." Our culture articulated that preposterous idea in an infamous line from a certain blockbuster movie of the 90s: "You complete me." Nooooo! That's not how it works!

And yet. So many relationships I saw around me were based in this need to be made whole. On one level, yes, we do need to be made whole. By God. Not by a spouse. Putting a spouse in the role of completer forces on the spouse a standard and requirement that cannot be met. And you know what? Sex is powerful, but it just doesn't have that kind of wholeness-making power. Even in the context of a healthy marriage, sex cannot heal all my broken places. Sex cannot meet all my needs. If we rely upon sexual connection to be the catch-all answer, we are in for a world of hurt.

And, lest you thought I was done, here's yet another obstacle I had to climb over in order to get healed enough to even consider walking toward a relationship: the Church's idolization of marriage.

Yes, I said that.

It's fine to value and esteem this beautiful union God created. But not to idolize it. Not to communicate that if you get married, you will reach the ultimate goal of humanity. I've known so many single people who feel as though they are grossly cheated out of life if they don't have a spouse. Even much of Church culture focuses around married couples and families. It's easy to pick up the implicit message that marriage is more valuable than singleness. If you're single in the Church, you likely won't hear good conversation about healthy sexuality unless you're in a group for porn addiction or premarital counseling.

I've found that this is the most prominent message on sexuality taught in Church: Don't even think about it!

As you can see, I had plenty to wrestle with before even beginning to believe I could walk into marriage. By far the biggest of those obstacles was my understanding of the difference between lust and attraction and between lust and love. Actually, it was similar to wrestling through my same-sex struggle; I had to learn to understand the difference between being driven by my brokenness and needs and being driven by wholeness and a desire to connect.

I was about to learn that connection birthed out of admiration, appreciation, and being stirred by beauty was quite different from lusting after someone I envied who was never meant to meet or complement my heart in healthy union. I was also about to learn not to disqualify what I was feeling just because it didn't feel the same as the broken, distorted, yet familiar feelings of my past. If that is all you know, then that's what you think your target is. When I finally understood that what I would feel for a woman was probably going to be very different than what I had felt for men, a lot of the mystique, fear, and disqualification began to evaporate.

PSA: I know this is a lot more commentary than story right now, and with apologies to my high-school English teacher who kept saying, "Show, don't tell," I feel it's just as important to tell as to show in this case. And now, for the story.

So, we're back to young Drew who is questioning his capacity for romantic love with a woman.

Sure, I could find a woman beautiful. But would I feel sexual attraction to her? Would I feel drawn to or enticed by her? I had felt longings for sexual connection with other guys, but I had never felt that same sort of attraction or pull toward a woman.

Falling in love with Suzanne was very different.

I'm ashamed to admit it, but I don't remember the first time I met her. Humorously, at the time our paths first crossed, I was already in the process of trying to pursue another girl. And that attempt did not go well. Not only did

I not know what I was doing, but I was trying to date someone who was probably not ready to be in a relationship. The whole thing imploded before it even really got going anywhere. That kind of hurt my heart.

As Suzanne tells it, the first time we met was at a basketball game at the Portland college she and my brother were both attending. Because she was friends with my brother before she met me, it was a bit of a novelty for her to finally meet his twin brother. Apparently, we met and shook hands. We even had a picture taken together with my brother. I have absolutely no memory of any of this, because I was too busy seething and glaring at the girl who had just rejected me. Not a very glorious first meeting. But thank God that's not the end of the story.

A couple months later, I went over to my brother's place where he was hanging out with some friends. I'd come to his apartment to talk about some interesting developments in our family. At that point, our family was very fractured and broken, but I saw that the Lord was restoring relationships that deeply affected him. As I poured out my heart to my brother and watched the tears forming in his eyes, my attention shifted to a short brunette girl standing to his right. And I noticed tears in her eyes, too.

Those beautiful eyes.

For a moment I forgot what I was saying. As I watched tears well up in Suz's eyes as she listened to what I was saying, I was immediately struck at the depth of her empathy for my brother. Others in the room were listening, and they were visibly moved, but not like she was. It was the first time I saw a glimpse of the depth of this woman's heart. Suz has a heart so deep and so loyal and so loving that in that moment my breath was taken away at the simple glimpse of it.

I didn't know her name at the time, but she had already begun to capture my heart. That might sound dramatic, and it might sound unrealistic, but in that moment I felt something I never had felt before.

Did I mention she was also really beautiful? Long, brown hair, olive-colored skin, blue eyes that turn crystalline when she cried, and—oh yeah—she's only 5'1". That was super attractive to me, since I'm only 5'7". Standing next to her, I felt like a tall man (not a common experience for me). Anyway, there was just so much tenderness and love in her. She radiated safety, tenderness, and compassion. She was unafraid to show emotion, and she could feel deeply for someone else. She obviously cared about my brother and our situation. I saw and felt all of this in just one moment.

By the time I left my brother's place that night, though I hadn't even talked to her, the image of the beautiful brunette with the blue eyes and big heart haunted my thoughts wonderfully for the next several weeks. She was probably my motivation to spend an increasingly large amount of time with my brother and his friends.

A month or so later, with the same group of friends, I had another glimpse of the heart and soul of this woman.

A group of us had been hanging out watching *Survivor* and sharing dinner. After the show, several people left for worship team practice. Only about four of us remained. The beautiful brunette was one of them. After sitting awkwardly for a few moments on the couch, while another show continued, I decided to get up and begin working on the mountain of dishes. A few minutes into the washing, I noticed that someone had come up beside me at the sink—without a word—to help me. It was her.

Again, I don't know how to communicate what happened in my heart at that moment. There is nothing about what I was experiencing that felt lustful or even erotic, and so I didn't know how to identify the feelings welling up inside of me, other than just to sit in awe of them. As she stood next to me doing the dishes, her arm brushed up against mine. Just for a second. I felt like my knees were going to give out. And I didn't understand that. There's nothing sexy about washing dishes. But somehow, by simply standing next to me, and with a brief touch of her arm against mine, she almost knocked me down.

The weirdest thought crossed my mind: "I wonder if she would want to do dishes with me for the rest of our lives?" I kid you not.

Not only was this mystery woman beautiful and deep and compassionate and empathetic, but she had a servant heart as well. No one had asked her to help me, and she didn't make a show of it. It was the most natural thing in the world for her to lend a hand to help. And so there we stood, silently doing the dishes, as things started awakening in me that I had never felt before.

The next time I saw her, a group of us went to see a movie. I was working full-time and wasn't part of the college that she and the rest of my brother's friends all attended, but I was vicariously living a college experience through them. We decided to see a movie that was staring a popular rap artist at the time. This was not a great movie choice, but my attention was absorbed in making sure I sat next to the beautiful brunette.

Did I mention she is beautiful? Did I mention her laugh is hysterical? That you can hear it from a mile away? Did I mention she doesn't know how to wink? Seriously. To wink she has to purposely and slowly concentrate and turn her head to the side. It is a full-face wink. It's adorable. But anyway, I made sure I was sitting next to her when the movie started.

If you've ever seen this movie, which I don't recommend, you'll know there is an extremely inappropriate scene in it. And what makes it even worse is that while it's happening, the musical soundtrack silences, and—without any distractions—you see and hear... very inappropriate things. There is nothing to camouflage it. It is just right there in front of you—magnified on a massive screen. As all good Christians would, everyone in our group felt the distinct awkwardness of the moment and the urge to try to mitigate it.

I didn't want to watch the scene, but there was no escaping it. And worse, I was sitting right next to the girl that I was increasingly interested in and wanted to potentially pursue a relationship with. Great move, Drew! You took her to a movie that is defiling us! Way to go!

As I sat there in the theater, trying to look down, or sideways, a hand came up and pulled the side of my face to the left. I was now facing Suz, who was shielding both of our eyes as we looked at each other instead of the spectacle playing out on the screen.

She smiled. "Well this is kind of awkward, isn't it?"

The film melted away in that moment. She was adorable. She wasn't afraid to steer headlong into the awkward to protect my integrity. And she was making an unbearable moment bearable—a skill she has continually practiced with mastery in our sixteen years together.

As I am recalling these memories, I'm overwhelmed by gratitude to the Lord for putting this incredible woman in my life. And I'm also once again feeling very vulnerable. Over the years, our relationship has been attacked many times. We have been criticized and mocked. She has been judged for marrying me. We've been told that our marriage is a sham or a fraud and that I am a self-hating gay who is trying to repress my feelings and hiding in this marriage.

I do *not* hate myself. But I *do* hate all that invective and assumption. If I hadn't struggled with same-sex attraction, then this love story I'm telling wouldn't be viewed with a lot of scrutiny. But if history is any predictor, I know how some people will interpret my relationship. Hence my vulnerability as I write this: that the moment Suz shielded my eyes with her hands, I began to fall in love with her. The desire to pursue her became stronger than the fear of failure or rejection that arose when I thought about stepping into a heterosexual relationship. It even became stronger than a new fear: the fear that she would reject me because of my past.

After the movie, the whole group went to a local coffee shop, and I sat there with my coffee, looking at this woman and wondering if I even had a shot with her. The rest of the evening, I let my heart dream of loving her and being loved by her. I wondered what our lives could look like together and how we might serve the Lord together and how we might grow old together. Strangely, not once did my thoughts veer toward lust or lustful fantasy. Not once did I sexualize her. And this might sound strange, but that upset me; I questioned whether my feelings were valid or real.

Our culture shortcuts so quickly to sex. "Sexual compatibility" has become a determining factor for whether a relationship will last or is worth committing to. This necessitates having sex long before commitment. I can tell you right now this is *not* God's heart for any of us. Not to say that erotic love is unimportant in marriage, but healthy erotic love should grow and flourish within the commitment of marriage. It should grow out of safety and out of security. Erotic love is not a bad thing at all—it's actually a very good thing in the right context. But it is heartbreaking for me to remember that I felt discouraged because erotic love wasn't my first feeling toward Suzanne.

Honestly? I wanted to be with her. I wanted to know her. I wanted to live my life with her. I was falling in love with her. And all this before we even had our first date. But there is an unhealthy expectation that eros is supposed to be the first—or the main—motivator toward marriage. I think this is more a reflection of collective sexual brokenness than a reflection of God's design or heart for us.

When Suz and I finally did have a first date, we went to one of our favorite spots in Southeast Portland, a coffee and dessert house in Ladd's Addition. As we sat and enjoyed dessert, Suzanne asked me to share my testimony with her. I felt simultaneously terrified and excited. I wanted her to know me, and here was the invitation to share what the Lord had walked me through. I didn't hold back. I shared all of it. As I spoke, I scanned her face to see if she was repulsed by or afraid of what I was sharing. Not once did I see a hint of rejection or fear. Instead, all I saw were those beautiful blue eyes, sometimes filling with tears, and sometimes squinting with her smile. She was fully engaged the entire time. At the end of the evening, I dropped her off and went home. When my roommates asked me how it went, I didn't hesitate. I said, "She has two choices: She's either going to marry me or break my heart."

I don't know how I had so much clarity. I know it sounds kind of crazy. But I just knew. I had found someone whom my heart loved. She had won my heart, and I was willing to risk everything to win *her* heart.

Thirteen months later, I stood at the front of a church and watched my beautiful, snarky, amazing, wonderful, ridiculously strong Suzanne walk down the aisle to become my wife. Surrounded by our friends and family—people who fully knew our story and the beauty of redemption it held— we worshipped God and pledged our lives to one another. As I write this, we've now been married for almost fifteen years, and we are raising three beautiful daughters together.

Suz still has the most beautiful eyes I've ever seen.

She still has the most magnificent heart I've ever encountered.

I love her with all my heart. Our life together and our love together is rich. And all the fears I once had about my capacity to love a woman romantically, sexually, passionately—all those fears have been silenced by the great gift of God that is Suzanne.

And you know how God works things for good? Turns out, there was a great benefit to walking through what I did before entering marriage; the relationship Suz and I built did not start with the shaky foundation of erotic love. It wasn't based on sexual attraction, although it very much included it. It was based on deep, abiding, multi-faceted love. And because of that sure foundation, erotic love could grow in a strong, sheltered, committed place.

I have worked in pastoral ministry for over a decade and a half. I can tell you that any marriage based on infatuation, sexual attraction, and erotic love will hit some really hard times when circumstances in life make you feel less sexy. Suz and I have had three children. There were seasons in pregnancy and post-pregnancy when the last thing on Suz's mind was sexual intimacy. She didn't feel attractive, and she didn't want any of that business. And I don't blame her. When I was trying to finish college while also raising kids and working full time, I was stressed and didn't feel much desire, either. Suz and I have faced conflicts and brokenness in our family, we've wrestled through seasons of sadness and disappointment, and we've faced injury and illness. In those times, sexual intimacy wasn't flourishing.

One example: When our oldest daughter was five years old, she was hospitalized for over a month. At the same time, we had just bought a foreclosure home and were fixing it up to move into. With all the emotional, financial, and physical stress of that season, sex was the last thing on either of our minds. If our relationship had been based on sexual compatibility or infatuation, that season would've killed it for sure.

Here's the thing about Suzanne: She's my best friend. She's my favorite person. She's my partner in crime. Some seasons of our life together have really been hard—even painful. That comes with life and marriage. But even in those seasons, we often look at each other and say, "There's no one I'd rather have it suck with than you."

We have weathered a lot, and we probably will continue to weather a lot in the future. I'm so grateful that our foundation is love, that our relationship is centered in God's will, and that one of the hallmarks of our relationship is that we push each other to become more like Jesus. I am grateful that our story is a story of redemption. I'm grateful that our relationship submits to and honors the Word of God. I am grateful that we continue to push each to be more and more as Christ made us to be. I'm grateful that we love each other out of the overflow of our hearts instead of trying to "complete" each other.

There's a beautiful resonance in our relationship, one that I believe only happens when you're walking as God made you. And I truly believe God made us for each other. There is something incredibly beautiful about the complementary nature of God's design of male and female. They can be physically complementary, emotionally complementary, and spiritually complementary. It is a divine relationship. In my experience, homosexual relationship just doesn't match it.

Chapter 9

The Wedding

Some people might have been surprised to receive my wedding invitation. I wasn't surprised when I received my brother's. I haven't mentioned it yet, but my brother embraces a homosexual identity.

How to respond? How would I—a man who had formerly lived in a homosexual relationship, who was now in a heterosexual marriage, and had an ex-gay ministry—respond to a same-sex marriage invitation?

I'll get back to that question, but I'm going to take the long way around.

Let me start with this controversial statement: I believe you can attend the wedding ceremony of two people of the same sex without celebrating or approving the union.

It seems ridiculous to me that I even have to make that statement. I know many people debate this issue constantly, and they have intellectual and theological reasons for their positions. But I don't know many people who consider the motivation of a person attending a same-sex wedding.

In conservative Christian culture, when people start talking about homosexuality, objectivity and context seem to go right out the window. If you don't have homosexual friends or family, that might not be an issue for you. But for those of us who have to relationally deal with this in the context of our own families and communities, objectivity is pretty darn important. These are not just abstract ideas or hypothetical questions to ponder; they are incarnated with faces, names, and identities.

My grandpa used to say: "It's easy to be a holy man on a hilltop." In other words, the elevated viewpoint when you're up above the trenches of the valley can be pretty unrealistic. It's easy to pass down judgment and declare platitudes from way up there because you do not have any skin in the game. But when you're down in the depths, those proclamations from the hilltop don't make one bit of sense at best, and at worst, they cause pain and damage.

For me, the issue of homosexuality and gay marriage is not just a concept, and it's not an abstraction. It is not a relational hypothetical. It is something I am personally wrestling with way down in the valley. On a personal level, it has been a central struggle I have contended with. I had to decide whether or not I would choose to surrender my sexual desires to Christ in a mainstream culture that criticized such an attempt and in a church culture that has been impotent and compromising regarding sexual ethics.

Once I managed to walk through all that, I began ministering to men and women who were struggling to do the same thing. Their lives and their choices and the constant battle in their hearts to remain faithful to Jesus—that was my day-in and day-out vocation.

When I talk about homosexual struggle and gay marriage, many real faces and stories inform my perspective. I think of parents of loved ones. Of families who are now estranged because of the tension created by this issue. Of prodigal sons and daughters, and parents waiting at the end of the road for their return. I've seen and heard so much heartache and frustration and hopelessness. Heaped on that is the tangible weight of judgment and condemnation these families feel. And the saddest part? That judgment and condemnation mostly comes from other Christians.

I am not at all being dramatic here (and I am the first one to tell you I can be dramatic). Still, I can get emotional when I talk about these things. I *am* emotional when I talk about these things, because I have seen the heartache. I've seen brokenness and rejection and frustration as a direct result of the condemnation and judgment passed down from people who are detached from this issue. And I have seen firsthand how the consequences of not dealing well with these relational dynamics ends up spreading beyond individual families and greatly affecting the Body of Christ.

Nevertheless, let me take a moment to be clear about something. I do not judge anyone in the Christian faith who holds a different conviction on the "do or do not go to the wedding" debate. This is a very complex issue. Many Christians are simply trying to remain faithful to what they believe the Bible is telling them to do. I do not doubt the convictions of these individuals at all. Hear me: If the conclusions I draw on this topic are different from your own, please, let's not judge each other. I believe it is absolutely possible to graciously and mercifully disagree without condemnation. Unfortunately, that is not always what Christians are known for.

Allow me to share my perspective by telling you about Matt and Will.

I'll start with Matt. Matt and I have one of the most complex relationships possible; we are identical twins. Any twins will know what I'm talking about. My brother and I have been through hell together, and we have put each other through hell. We have worked out innumerable interpersonal conflicts together. Sometimes the working out of these conflicts was, um, less than mature—or even civilized. We both bear the emotional and physical scars as evidence of our "working it out."

As kids, we were just as likely to stab each other with forks as we were to have each other's backs. Sometimes the fork stabbing happened *while* having the other's back. My wife once described the relationship to our friends like this: "I have never seen two people love each other more fiercely and yet contend with each other so powerfully all at the same time." If sibling relationships can be complex and convoluted, twin relationships can be exceedingly so. For the majority of my life, Matt has been my best friend, my closest confidant—and my nemesis! Yeah, it's complicated. Bottom line: I love my brother with all my heart.

It was after Matt watched my own journey out of homosexuality—and after he stood as the best man in my wedding—that my brother came out as gay.

I understand the kind of pain and struggle he was experiencing. I know what it is to fear rejection, and I know the religious environment we were both steeped in. The stakes were sky-high for him when he came out. When he did, I am ashamed to say that my reaction was less than gracious and certainly less empathetic than it could've been.

Like many family members of those who come out and identify as LGBTQ, I felt an enormous pressure to try to convince my brother to choose otherwise. I took on the role of Holy Spirit and tried to lead him into conviction. I felt confused, hurt, betrayed, and I wanted to fix it. In my own grief and frustration, I did things and said things that hurt my relationship with my brother—things that effectively reduced him to a problem to fix, not a person to love. I can tell you right now that this is not an effective strategy. It was incredibly unfair to him, and it wasn't very loving. It was, however, a very common response.

If someone in your family announces a gay identity, remember this; although that may be new information to you, it is not at all new for the person who finally discloses it. They have likely been struggling with this identity for a long, long time. When they tell you, "I'm gay," that is no flippant whim. Whether a person is announcing a struggle with homosexuality or an established identity with homosexuality, the issue has likely been building for years by the time they say anything.

Although I wanted to be able to change my brother's ideas of his identity, by the time he told me, he was already set in a trajectory toward this reality. And it wasn't long before that new reality included Matt's partner, Will.

When Matt introduced Will to our family—or more accurately, when Matt introduced the reality that there even was a Will out there—it was a total game-changer for Suz and me. When Matt told us about his homosexuality, it was still in the realm of ideas. But when Matt spoke Will's name and announced that he was moving to our town to join my brother in his life, ideas took on tangible human form. Matt told us how kind Will was and how he was sure we would like him. Honestly? All those words were lost on me. Not because they weren't true, but because Will represented finality. He represented a total shift in the dynamics of the relationship between my brother and me. He represented a new reality that we could not ignore but had to face.

An additional twist to the story is that Matt and Will both identify as gay Christians. This complicated things for Suz and me quite significantly. How do we respond to professing Christians who embrace gay behavior or gay relationship? Does the teaching from 1 Corinthians 5:11—to not even eat with such a man (the sexually immoral brother in Christ)—mean that I now can no longer share a dinner with my brother? Does not having fellowship with someone who claims to be a Christian and yet walks in sexual brokenness mean I can no longer have my brother over to hang out and watch TV? Am I supposed to cut off relationship with my brother to lead him to repentance?

I have ministered to countless Christians over the years who have wrestled with this very thing. On top of that, they felt the sting of dogmatic judgement from fellow Christians whenever they struggled to implement the hard and fast "don't eat with such a man" rule with members of their immediate family. There is incredible pressure to be faithful to this teaching so as to not celebrate sin. This puts families into the dilemma of whether to choose to honor God or choose to be disobedient. Supposedly, the only way to honor God in this scenario is to effectively reject and cut off your loved one.

I have watched numerous family members choose to either abandon their faith or to twist their entire theology on this topic so they don't have to reject their loved one. And I have watched numerous families reject and alienate their loved one, hoping that this would lead their LGBTQ family member to repentance, only to see them run further away from God and become more firmly embedded and entrenched in relationships that affirm their sexual identity. And those are the best-case scenarios. I have also heard and

126

seen the damage and pain to the LGBTQ person, and we have all heard the high statistics of homelessness and suicide in the LGBTQ community due to the profound sense of loss and rejection they feel from family members who are often operating under the assumption that the Bible says we need to cut off and cast out. Because that's what leads people to repentance, right?

Or maybe we've been missing something.

Let's examine the passage in 1 Corinthians 5 that started all of this.

> I wrote to you in my letter not to *associate* with sexually immoral people—not at all meaning the sexually immoral of this world, or the greedy and swindlers, or idolaters, since then you would need to go out of the world. But now I am writing to you not to *associate* with anyone who bears the name of brother if he is guilty of sexual immorality or greed, or is an idolater, reviler, drunkard, or swindler—not even to eat with such a one (1 Corinthians 5:9–11, emphasis mine).

Paul was addressing the Corinthian church and calling them into repentance and correction. A man in the church was having a sexual relationship with his father's wife, presumably his step-mother. And the church was celebrating and boasting about it. Paul rightly calls this boasting into account and instructs the church to deal severely with the man in their congregation. This was church discipline. Paul's motivation here was larger than just the one man's sin; it was also about the effect that boasting about this man's inclusion in the fellowship would have on the Church body and how celebrating the sin was corrupting the church in Corinth.

The Greek word *synanamignymi* is usually translated as "associate" or "mix."[4] The ESV translation above uses "associate." We also find this word in the Septuagint (LXX: the Greek translation of the Old Testament), in the context of maintaining the purity and holiness of Israel.

For example (with emphasis mine), Hosea 7:8 (LXX) translates it: "Ephraim, he hath *mixed* himself among the people; Ephraim is a cake not turned." And, Ezekiel 20:18 (LXX) translates it: "Do not walk in the statutes of your fathers, nor observe their ordinances and in their ways do not *mix* and defile yourselves." From these passages we can see that this word relates to ungodly mixture with the sinful ways of the prevalent culture.

In the first century, Paul felt great concern that believers were being led astray, and their holiness was getting "mixed" with the paganistic, permissive, sinful, idolatrous culture around them. Paul was not just calling the sexually sinful man to repentance, but also the church that was celebrating his sin. It makes sense that Paul would use the word he did, because it carried the historical implication of the pollution of Israel—who had also mixed among sinful people, as referenced in the Hosea verse.

We also have to look at the injunction: "Don't even eat with such a man." Was this a corporate mandate, an individual mandate, or both? Much of the Church says it's both. Even my initial response to Matt was to not associate with my brother to the extent that I could "not even eat" with such a man. Consequently, I cut off my brother and Will.

---

[4] *Strong's Exhaustive Concordance*, s.v. *"Synanamignymi"* (Greek #48); https://www.blueletterbible.org/lang/lexicon/lexicon.cfm?Strongs=G4874&t=ESV.

I thought I had no other option if I wanted to remain in right standing with God and my Christian community.

A long time passed. Suz and I grieved heavily. I was deeply unsettled during this season, wondering if we had interpreted that Scripture correctly, if we had discerned a good application, and if we had done the right thing.

And then we began to wonder: Maybe there was another way to respond to Matt and Will that was biblically faithful, unswervingly truthful, aligned with our convictions, but also left room for some sort of relationship. There *had* to be! Because the reality of what we were living didn't feel like it was accurately representing the character of Christ. It also seemed to be inconsistently applied in the Church. Now, that is no reason to reject the interpretation. Failure to live up to a teaching doesn't mean it is wrong. But it was deeper than that.

I went to the Lord, and to the Word—not just to the opinions or interpretations of others in the Christian community.

I could not escape the fact that the context of 1 Corinthians 5 was corporate correction. There were also so many ties to communion around the passage, that I began to wonder if "eating with" had more to do with communion, or if eating together carried with it a cultural significance for the early Church that doesn't easily translate to our current culture. It was then that I learned about love feasts. We can find reference to these in Jude 12, and they are recorded as an integral part of Church life, worship, and fellowship into the second and third centuries. The following is from the definition of love feast from the *Evangelical Dictionary of Biblical Theology:*

The term chosen to describe it reveals that it was to be an event in which love was expressed and fellowship confirmed. In the Greco-Roman or Jewish household of that day sharing in a meal signified acceptance and fellowship, and the love feast in the church was to be a living example of unity. That this unity was a very serious matter can be seen in that the love feast is mentioned in the context of a denunciation of false teachers and admonishment of the congregation. The significance of the event was such that the unhindered participation of false believers in the love feasts, which signified their acceptance into the fellowship, was a "blemish" or taint on the event and also a danger for the church...

The church order of Hippolytus, which is much later than the New Testament, gives the fullest description of what had come to be called the agape. It consisted of a meal that was taken by believers at someone's house or in the church and was presided over by a church officer (normally the bishop). Ignatius, in his letter to the Smyrneans, may give evidence that the love feast and communion were closely connected: "It is not lawful apart from the bishop either to baptize or to hold a love-feast [agape]" (see Ignatius, To the Romans 7). However, Tertullian's description is of a communal meal, which begins with prayer, followed by people eating and drinking, the singing of hymns, and a closing prayer....[5]

These love feasts eventually diminished and died out by the third century. (For the record, I do not believe the modern church potluck holds a candle to the potency, intimacy, or unity represented in this tradition.)

---

[5] Walter A. Elwell, *Evangelical Dictionary of Biblical Theology* (Ada, MI: Baker Books, 1998).

After discovering this tradition, I started thinking: Maybe "don't eat with" could be interpreted as "do not share deep spiritual fellowship with" or more specifically, "do not celebrate a love feast with such a man." It makes sense that the apostle Paul would forbid sharing the kind of fellowship and unity represented and affirmed in the love feast with someone who has adopted immorality as good and right. I agree with that completely, and in that context, it makes more sense of the commandment to not mix or associate with the sexually immoral. With that in mind, maybe I can grab lunch with my twin brother and not enrage God Almighty. Maybe families can invite their gay loved ones who still claim Jesus to Thanksgiving dinner without violating Scripture and bringing the judgement of God down on their households. Relationship does not have to presuppose agreement, or even moral unity, or else Paul would not have given us the option to relate to the unsaved sinner.

As I began to consider this, another New Testament passage began to inform my thoughts. In 2 Thessalonians 3:14–15, Paul makes the same statement about not mixing or associating with a disobedient believer. Again, he uses the Greek word *synanamignymi*, but in the 2 Thessalonians occurrence, the ESV translates it as "to do with." The instruction is similar. But notice my emphasis in verse 15:

> If anyone does not obey what we say in this letter, take note of that person, and have nothing to do with him, that he may be ashamed. *Do not regard him as an enemy, but warn him as a brother* (2 Thessalonians 3:14–15).

The J.B. Phillips version puts it this way:

> If anyone refuses to obey the command given above, mark that man, do not associate with him until he is

ashamed of himself. *I don't mean, of course, treat him as an enemy, but reprimand him as a brother.*

To reprimand is to tell someone that his or her behavior is wrong and unacceptable. The injunction here is: Don't treat the person as an enemy; reprimand him as a brother. This seems to imply that "not mixing" or "not associating" does not necessarily mean "have no relationship with." After all, you can't reprimand someone as a brother if you have shunned and rejected relationship with them.

After much prayer and counsel, and after time wrestling in the Word, Suz and I made the decision to contact my brother. He and I had a long, painful, and honest conversation. I am happy to report that no one was stabbed with a fork during the conversation. I reaffirmed my convictions: I believed that his relationship with Will was foundationally outside of the design and will of God and thus was sin. I shared that this conviction was not going to change. I shared that my hope in breaking relationship with him had been to move him to repentance. We both shared how we had hurt each other in our processing. I asked my brother for forgiveness for rejecting him and trying to manipulate him into repentance.

I repented to my brother.

That conversation was a tightrope walk—on an incredibly precarious tightrope, hundreds of stories above spiked concrete and a tank of sharks with lasers on their heads. In repenting to my brother, there was no way I could repent of my convictions. I just couldn't. I believe his relationship with Will is sin. Still, that didn't mean I handled my relationship with the two of them correctly just because of the rightness of my theology. It didn't mean the application of the truth relationally was very loving. In my attempt to win the argument and turn my brother from his sin, I made him a problem to fix, not a person to love. That is never loving.

It was humbling to admit I had wronged him in this process. But the simple truth is that I had, and I needed to repent of that and ask forgiveness for the hurt I had caused him.

I also felt immense pressure because of my position in ministry. I knew people were going to see my actions and my choices regarding my brother, and I knew some would judge me for my decision to reconnect in relationship and to accept Will as part of my brother's life. Not only that, but making space for relationship with my brother and Will—without changing my convictions about the sinful nature of homosexual behavior—meant I was going to be relating to two people who knew that Suz and I believe their behavior and relationship is inherently sinful.

This was not going to be insta-happily-ever-after for any of us. One twin was in ex-gay ministry, the other was in a gay relationship. I was choosing to connect with a gay family member within a belief system that saw that as wrongful condoning, and Matt was choosing to connect with someone who was actively involved in a ministry he deeply, deeply disagreed with. This was uncharted territory for all of us.

Ultimately our decision was that we were going to do whatever it took to be able to walk out our relationship in love, honesty, acceptance, and disagreement. Over the next few years, we grew in our ability to have honest conversation, to navigate offenses, to step into very tense and unresolvable conflicts, and yet to choose to love each other through it.

When Suzanne and I begin having kids, we had even more territory to navigate.

I ministered to parents who asked what to say to their children when loved ones brought a partner home. They would look at me and ask, "Well, you have kids, and your brother is gay, and he's partnered, how do you handle it with your kids?"

There is no special-formula answer. Uncle Matt was Uncle Matt, and we made the decision that Will was Uncle Will. Our kids have a lot of "uncles" and "aunts" who are not biological, but who earned that distinction because they are loved, trusted people in our lives, and they love and invest in our kids well. They are people of presence in our lives. Matt is biologically Uncle Matt, but Will—he has earned the title of Uncle Will. He has been a presence in our kids' lives from the moment they were born. I mean that literally. Matt and Will were there at the birth center the day our daughter Olivia was born. Of all the pictures we took that day, Uncle Will probably had the biggest smile on his face when he held Olivia. He and Matt love our girls fiercely. They are family to us. It seems stupid to even have to say that. Of course they are family to us! Regardless of the fact that we have a deep disagreement spiritually and morally, we are family.

It is possible to deeply disagree with someone at a fundamental level of spirituality and personhood, to not have those disagreements resolved, and yet still be committed to loving them. Yes, it's difficult, but it feels so much more like the heart of Jesus than walking away from them.

A prominent Christian theologian and speaker once told me that I was being disobedient to God in my relationship with my brother and Will because I was not willing to do the difficult thing of breaking relationship with them. He told me

I was taking the comfortable and easy way out. I *wholeheartedly* disagree. It would be easier to *not* relate to them, to ignore the reality of Will, to reject them both and piously hide behind the "rightness" of my position and my "holiness." Not only is that easier, but it also feeds a deep sense of self-righteousness and superiority (not good colors on any believer, by the way).

Cutting them off and casting them out could have relieved a lot of tension. I wouldn't have to relationally deal with conflict, and I wouldn't have to walk the tightrope of truth and love. Also, I wouldn't have to wrestle deeply with my own convictions and presumptions. No doubt, it would be difficult to walk through the pain of separation, but not nearly as difficult as it can be to remain in relationship through every conflict, every disagreement, every moment of tension, and every disappointment. Not to mention enduring the harsh judgements of many in the Church.

But if Scripture is any model, if you are going to try to love people like Jesus did, you are going to get judged, and your reputation is going to be called into question. You are going to deal with betrayal and rejection. You are going to experience abandonment and misrepresentation. If it happened to Jesus, it will happen to us. In fact, maybe this should be a litmus test for Christians. Maybe, if you are not pissing off the religious norm by choosing to eat with the "sinners" (not to celebrate their behavior but to love them), you are not resembling Jesus enough. Yeah. I just said that.

Choosing to be in relationship with Matt and Will meant that Suz and I were inevitably going to face the decision that looms in the minds and hearts of anyone who holds the same convictions we do and has loved ones in the LGBTQ community. The decision of attending the wedding.

Cue ominous, suspense filled music.

Matt and Will were in a relationship for many years before the marriage conversation came up. Marriage meant wedding. And attending the wedding was a decision I was dreading.

Full disclosure; I didn't want to go. I was already on the business end of judgement from some in the Christian community for simply staying in relationship with my brother and Will. If simply eating dinner with Matt was an issue, attending his wedding ceremony was going to be a doozy. I could see the pitchforks and torches. Added to that external questioning was my own internal version: How could I affirm or celebrate this choice?

When we first began having the conversations about the wedding with Matt and Will, Suzanne and I kept saying, "Matt, Will, we are so sorry, but we cannot go to your wedding. We just cannot celebrate this with you." It was probably fortunate that we began having these conversations over a year in advance. It gave us all time to process. Nevertheless, it was something that Suz and I wrestled with and felt deeply conflicted over.

Let me tell you something about Suzanne here. She is one of the most fiercely loyal lovers of people I've ever met in my life. She would probably disagree with that statement, because she's also very much an introvert. But regardless of her introverted nature, she loves with her whole heart. Once you are in that heart of hers, you are in! She will fight for you with a relentless patience and a depth that resembles God more than anyone else I have ever met. (She probably needs this characteristic to be married to me!) Suzanne had known my brother Matt for at least a year and a half before she met me; he was already a big brother to her before she and I began to date. And all of that was way before my brother came out as gay. All that to say, the prospect of not being at his wedding gutted her. It gutted me, too.

All this pain and frustration led me to another internal wrestling match—similar to the one I'd had when I began to question the party-line interpretation of "don't eat with such a man." This time, my opponent in the ring was the mandate: "Don't be caught dead at a gay wedding."

At the crux of this debate is the issue of celebration or approval. We've all heard the argument that no Christian in good conscience—being committed to a biblical understanding of marriage, sexuality, and sin—can celebrate a gay union. I agree. We cannot celebrate sin. I would even go a step further to say that we need to examine whether, by our passivity and silence, we may appear to celebrate or approve of this type of union. It's cheating to say, "Well, they know I am Christian, so they must know where I stand." That is no longer the case. Pro-gay theological interpretation has so infiltrated the Church that it is necessary to communicate our stance on such points of belief. Passivity and silence can and will be interpreted as approval.

But I *disagree* with the idea that a person's attendance at a gay wedding unequivocally communicates celebration or approval of the union between people of the same sex.

Scripture repeatedly shows us that God does not look merely at the external; He knows the heart. And God has consistently used His people in pagan cultures and contexts. One of my favorite examples is Daniel. Many Christians have said that the call recounted in the Book of Daniel to bow down to idols and forsake the worship of the one true God is like baking a cake for a gay couple or attending a same-sex wedding. Yet we forget that Daniel, Shadrach, Meshach, and Abednego lived and served in a pagan kingdom. In the midst of paganism, idolatry, sorcery, and wickedness, they managed to serve the reigning kingdom *and* maintain their integrity and favor with God.

We would never say that Daniel was guilty of celebrating idolatry or divination merely because he was held in respect by the king or because he was made the chief of the magicians, enchanters, Chaldeans, and astrologers (Daniel 5:11–12). We understand that while performing his tasks, Daniel remained surrendered to God, dependent on God, faithful to God, and blameless before God (Daniel 6:22). So how is it possible that we can understand that Daniel—as the appointed chief over those who performed witchcraft—can be found blameless before God, yet we cannot sit in a pew at a gay wedding without being guilty of celebrating sin?

This sounds similar to the way the Church condemns same-sex attraction as sin because of the type of temptation it is. As with that condemnation, Christians often lose their sense of reason whenever you raise the issue of homosexuality; heaven forbid you suggest that you can attend a same-sex wedding without betraying Jesus! And yet I know parents who sat at the heterosexual wedding of their son or daughter, deeply disagreeing with the union that was taking place, but choosing to be there regardless. Plenty of people knew their presence wasn't celebrating or approving, but no one told them they were betraying Jesus by being there.

As I was sweating through this theological wrestling match, I had the opportunity to share breakfast with a man of God I greatly respect. In fact, he is a genuine hero of the faith. It was a rare moment when we were both in the same state, and it worked out that we could spend some time together before he flew back home. Although we haven't had many face-to-face interactions, this man has had an immense impact on my life, and I consider him one of my most significant mentors. After some light and encouraging catching up, the conversation turned to greater depth. I began sharing my anguish about Matt and Will's wedding. And somehow, in a brief conversation with this man, who has one of the most intimate relationships with God I've ever seen, I was able to clearly see the heart of God for me in this decision. The simple takeaway: God, by His Holy Spirit, knew my situation, and He would give me grace to make my own decision. In fact, He gave me permission and blessing to do so.

A few weeks later, Suzanne and I were at dinner with Matt and Will at a restaurant in Northwest Portland when the wedding conversation came up again. In a moment of vulnerability, my brother asked, "I know you don't agree with our choice, but could you please just come? I can't imagine you not there."

He had tears in his eyes—genuine tears. As his twin, I know him better than well, and I knew he was not asking from a place of manipulation but from a place of love. He was asking his brother and sister-in-law to be present with him on the day he married.

For several years, Suz and I had known we'd have to make this decision. The longer my brother and Will were together, the likelier it became. I knew in my spirit that this was the moment of decision. All other talks had led to this one. We were down to raw vulnerability on all sides.

This was going to be a very consequential decision; if we chose not to go, our absence would negatively impact our relationship with Matt and Will. If we chose to go, there would be other consequences. I had surrendered my own homosexual struggle in obedience to Christ, and at that point, I had been in full-time ministry for eight years, helping people walk out of homosexuality. Our decision to attend or not attend my brother's gay wedding would impact our own family, but also the other families I ministered to. Could our decision negatively impact others? Would it negatively impact Portland Fellowship, the ministry where I was then on staff?

Holy Spirit graciously revealed two things to me in the moment Matt asked me that heavy question. First, Matt and Will knew and understood our disagreement with their choice. They knew that if we attended their wedding, it would be as an act of love toward them, not an act of agreement, celebration, or approval. Second, choosing to love my brother was not an offense against God.

And so, to the shock of my brother, Will, and Suzanne, I looked at Matt across the table, and with tears in my eyes said, "Yeah. We will be there."

Flash forward to the wedding day. I will never forget sitting in the row of white folding chairs in the middle of a hazelnut orchard, watching Matt and Will get married. Making the decision to sit in those seats had been a difficult journey for Suzanne and me, but as we sat there, we knew beyond a shadow of a doubt that God had led us to this decision. What looked like just passively sitting in folding chairs was one of the most conscious acts of our lives.

It wasn't just a difficult journey for Suz and me. As the minister opened the ceremony, she shared these words: "We know there are those of you here who do not agree with this union, yet you have made the choice to be here because you love Matt and Will, and for that, they thank you." As difficult as it was for us, I know it was painful for them to recognize our difficulty and to acknowledge it on their wedding day. Doing so was extremely gracious of them.

Why do I share this story? It still hurts all of my family. It also garners caustic reactions from people who hear of it. Attending a gay wedding is a polarizing choice, and critics seem to forget that real people with hearts are making that choice—and living with the consequences.

I share our story because I believe it is instructive. I share it because Matt, Will, Suzanne, and I—who have fought to have an honest, respectful, and loving relationship with one another, respecting our differences and accepting our disagreements—agree that it's worth sharing if it can help other families find permission to relate. Maybe relationships between family members that are already strained by differing worldviews *can* find a way to not fracture beyond repair.

I also share our story because it offers a missing perspective in the seemingly endless debate over whether a Christian who believes same-sex behavior is sin can, in good conscience, attend the wedding of two people of the same sex. In fact, I think it extends beyond just the wedding. I think this story helps inform whether a Christian can provide a service like baking a cake or arranging flowers for such an event without violating their faith.

(I'd like to note; this is different than the ongoing legal battle concerning freedom of religious practice. It's a big difference to examine the question of whether a Christian *can* engage—what I'm talking about here—than it is to fight the onslaught that a Christian *must* concede. Those concerned with these issues need to acknowledge that although the two are closely tied, they are *not* the same.)

Your turn. Say you're invited to a gay wedding. Do you fall into the "Jesus ate with sinners, so just go and love them" camp or the "No one who calls themselves a Christian would ever be caught dead at a gay wedding" camp? Or does neither extreme seem right to you?

Essentially, this dilemma is seen as a black and white one: You either celebrate or you don't celebrate. But that's not really the case. I can be present at an event without celebrating it.

To celebrate something is to rejoice in it, to praise it, to act with uninhibited joy and endorsement of it. Synonyms for *celebrate* include *commend, laud, glorify,* or *applaud.* If Suzanne and I were celebrating my brother's wedding, then the minister would not have felt the need to speak those opening words of recognition. Clearly, we were not commending, endorsing, glorifying, applauding, or praising the event. Our presence was not the same as celebration. We understood that, my brother and Will understood that, and most important to this conversation, God understood that.

We went to my brother's wedding. We demonstrated our unconditional love for him and Will. We showed them respect and value. We also had a lot of difficult and uncomfortable conversations leading up to the wedding, as I mentioned. Today, we accept that we cannot change their minds, and they accept that they cannot change ours. We know where we all stand: firmly in disagreement *and* love. So, is it possible to be at the ceremony but not be celebrating and "participating" in sin? Yes, I believe it is.

"But," you might ask, "what about the 'weaker brother' argument?"

I've heard that one in the context of gay weddings. It goes like this: Even if you could ensure that the couple marrying knew that you were not celebrating a union you did not agree with, what about the "weaker" Christian who might see you there "eating food sacrificed to idols" and have their faith compromised because they misunderstood your actions? (See 1 Corinthians 7.) This is an important argument to consider.

I acknowledge that our decisions do not just affect ourselves, but also the larger Body of Christ, yet I'm often amazed at the ridiculous solutions the Body of Christ throws at difficult issues. Great example: I read an article in which the author stated, incredulously, that if you could manage to ensure that the motive for your presence at a gay wedding was not approval or celebration, and that if you were actually there missionally (which he highly doubted was possible), then you had the responsibility to hide your decision from other believers because they could get confused and be led astray.

Really? *Really?*

In sad irony, faith is being shipwrecked and people are being led into heresy *because* this issue is not being talked about.

This plays out big time with parents of gay children. These parents see two choices: 1) Remain faithful to a traditional understanding of Scripture—with the attached assumption that they will not attend their own child's wedding—and possibly lose relationship with their child, or 2) Change their view of Scripture to keep in relationship with their children. Added to the complication is that many of these parents are pastors, professors, or leaders in the Church. When they are faced with this false dichotomy, often the kids win and the biblical truth loses as they alter theology to keep relationship.

Regarding this issue, a leader I respect greatly recently told me he thought I care primarily about relationships and that he cares primarily about the Church. I understand his concern. We both have watched the Church creep toward a liberal, compromised, and accommodating view of sexuality. Much of the language used to manipulate theology sounds familiar to me; it appeared in conversations with my brother. However, being willing to examine scriptural interpretation and come to different conclusions is hardly a new thing for the Body of Christ. Think about it: How many different Protestant denominations are there?

I considered my friend's concern for a long while. But here is a reality that anchors my convictions. Being concerned with relationships is the central concern of the gospel:

> "Love the Lord your God with all your heart and with all your soul and with all your mind and with all your strength." The second is this: "Love your neighbor as yourself." There is no commandment greater than these (Mark 12:30–31 NIV).

> A new command I give you: Love one another. As I have loved you, so you must love one another. By this everyone will know that you are my disciples, if you love one another (John 13:34–35 NIV).

These commandments are undeniably relational. Jesus wrapped up the entirety of the law and the prophets in the first two commandments and left us with only one new command in the Book of John: love one another. To be concerned with how we relate *is* to be concerned with the

Church. The Church is made of people who are exhorted to *relate* as Christ has commanded us. And if we don't know how to relate, we will *not* be strong, mature, or wise in leading the Church.

To those of you who have the son, daughter, brother, sister, or friend asking you to attend their same-sex wedding, know that God can lead you in your choice. He can give you the words to say. He can give you the grace to sit in a chair at the service. He can give you the grace to *not* sit in that chair. And even more important than that one service, God can give you the grace and the wisdom to get past that day and live the gospel by being incarnational in ongoing relationship with the person you love but whose lifestyle and choices you do not celebrate.

Suz and I love Matt and Will. They love us, too. Our relationship is intact. We may never agree. They may never change their minds and repent. Right now, they see nothing to repent of. But if they ever do, they will know we have always loved them and were present with them.

Choose to be present—maybe even at the wedding.

And now you might ask, "But what about the business owner who is asked for her product or service for a gay wedding?"

Allow me to share another story.

A good friend of mine is a professional musician in Portland, OR. Several months ago, during a conversation about all of this, I suggested that she think through how she would respond if a gay couple wanted to hire her for their wedding. A week after our conversation, a gay couple contacted her with that exact query. She called my wife and me and asked for our advice as to how to proceed. When the three of us met, I asked what her greatest fear or conflict was with the couple's request.

> Here is my paraphrase of her response: If I perform at their reception, I am worried they will believe I am OK with their marriage. I can't approve of their marriage, but I can't turn them down, because that is against the discrimination law. I don't want to lie and say I am already booked. I also don't want to be one more Christian who rejects them and pushes them further away from Jesus.

I think many Christians find themselves in this predicament. It seems to be a no-win situation. How do we not celebrate, approve, or endorse sin without rejecting people, violating the law, and pushing people away?

As Suz and I shared with our friend our decision-making process for attending my brother's wedding, we came up with a plan for how she could proceed with this couple. Later that week, she met with them and went over her contract, rates, song options, and time commitment. After all the standard contractual information was taken care of, she let them know she had something else she needed to discuss with them.

> This is, roughly, what she said: Before you hire me, I believe it is your right to know who you are hiring. In addition to being a professional musician, I am also a worship pastor at my church. I am a Christian, and I believe in traditional biblical marriage and sexuality. Because of that, I do not agree with gay marriage. If you do decide to hire me, I need you to know that you are hiring someone who could not and would not be agreeing or celebrating with you. I could not, in good conscience, allow you to hire me without you knowing that.

That being said, I also want you to know that as convicted as I am about my beliefs about marriage, I am also equally convicted in my belief that I am called to love my neighbor as myself. That call includes showing respect and kindness to those I do not agree with. I need you to know that if you do choose to hire me for your wedding, I will offer the same professional service I would to any other client. My performance will not reflect my lack of approval or celebration.

This is your wedding, and I felt you have a right to know that you were hiring someone who could not celebrate this day with you. You have the right to choose to hire someone else if that is important to you. I know this may complicate your decision to hire me or not. You do not need to answer me right now. Take whatever time you need.

In the end, they did not hire her. They did, however, thank her for her honesty and felt she handled the issue very respectfully. She did not violate state law by refusing to serve them, and she did not compromise the truth by not telling them of her beliefs.

What if they had hired her? She would have, in good conscience, been able to offer her service to them, knowing she had clearly communicated she did not agree with or celebrate their wedding. She would have also been representing Christ's incarnational love by choosing to serve those who do not agree with her and showing them a picture of God who is kind to those in sin and serves those who may very well reject Him—all while being a truthful witness who clearly communicated that her clients' choice was not in line with the commandments of the God she loves.

Even though she did not end up singing at the wedding, my friend may well have been one of the first examples of a Christian who did not reject or condemn this couple. Instead, she spoke truth to them in respect and love.

What if the incarnational gospel mission of Jesus can look like singing songs, or baking a cake, or even sitting in a white plastic folding chair?

Chapter 10

The Special Music Number

If you were part of evangelical church culture in the '90s, the following scenario may be familiar: The worship ends, and it's time to take the offering. As the pastor bows his head to pray and the ushers come down the aisles, someone moves to the platform, grabs the microphone, and quietly waits for the accompaniment track to start.

This, my friends, was the setup for what my childhood church called the *special music number*.

Though the setup and timing were the same every week, not all special music numbers were created equal. On good Sundays, the individual, duo, or group did a wonderful job; their voices blended, their spirits were humble, the song selection was appropriate, and the taped accompaniment only produced a slight hissing sound (versus the extreme hissing sound if the cassette tape had been worn out by over-use). In such moments, the special music number blessed the congregation and added wonderfully to the Sunday morning service.

But then (and you knew there'd be a "but then"!) there was the *other* kind of special music number. These were the Sundays when you opened your eyes after the pastor's offering prayer to see an individual or couple on the stage, and your first thought was, "Huh. I didn't know they could sing." And then the music started—probably Sandi Patti, Steve Green, or Amy Grant (pre-*Heart in Motion* Amy Grant, thank you very much). At this point, you may have thought, "Well, that's ambitious." And then the "singing" began. Over the next few moments of agony, your most noble thought was typically, "I really hope there are no visitors attending this morning!"

The most important task in such moments was what I called *face management*. This is the act of making sure that no matter the angst, torture, repulsion, or visceral discomfort you were struggling with on the inside, your face remained placid and agreeable on the outside. These were the unspoken rules of church during the "special" special music numbers. I always marveled at the pastoral staff's ability to endure these moments, particularly because both senior pastors of my childhood had musically talented families. They knew good music. And they knew bad music. And they could maintain a face that expressed, "Ah! What beautiful singing!" when we all knew darn well that it was "Ah...trocious!"

Thank God (and I am *not* taking His name in vain here), that such tests of endurance and character only lasted the length of a song. We all knew that in three to five minutes all would be well, and we could collectively move on. I will admit I learned something from these, um, performances: Bad singing did not necessarily represent the singer's heart. Those dear souls may have sounded like screaming goats getting slaughtered, but they could have internally been the most precious, humble, and pleasing offerings to the Lord. Conversely, the musical offering could have been delivered with perfect pitch, perfect rhythm, and perfect harmony, but the performer may have been full of pride and a complete lack of worship that was absolutely offensive to the Lord. Only the Lord knows the heart.

Why do I share this silly analogy? Well, for a while, during every Q&A portion of my teaching engagements, I was consistently being asked the same question: "What are your thoughts on Kim Davis?"

Now, there is a chance you may not know who Kim Davis is. Several years ago, she was all over the news cycle. Kim Davis served as a county clerk in Kentucky. After the Supreme Court decision to legalize same sex marriage in 2015, she was ordered by the governor of Kentucky to begin issuing marriage licenses to same-sex couples. This was a problem for her.

> Kim stated: I never imagined a day like this would come, where I would be asked to violate a central teaching of Scripture and of Jesus Himself regarding marriage. To issue a marriage license which conflicts with God's definition of marriage, with my name affixed to the certificate, would violate my conscience.

Kim defied the order. She was brought to court and ordered to comply, but she did not, citing that she was acting under the authority of God. She was then found in contempt of court, sent to jail for five days, and released with the order to issue the licenses. She created new licenses that did not bear her name, and she allowed other clerks in her office to issue those to same-sex couples. She has been demonized, caricatured, threatened, ridiculed, and jailed, all the while believing that to comply with the law would violate her conscience.

To be perfectly honest, I am deeply conflicted about Kim Davis—and about many others like her involved in the religious liberty aspect of this issue. For me, the most cringe-worthy part of the whole thing is the backlash from those with traditional views of marriage and sexuality. When I listen to these angry Christians, I feel like I'm back at a Sunday morning service sitting through a bad special music number, really hoping no visitors are watching and listening. Alas, unlike the special music number, this issue hasn't ended in three to five minutes.

Why has it become more important for some people in the Christian community to indignantly "defend the truth" about marriage than to lovingly represent the character of the One who made marriage?

I was reading through the Book of Matthew recently, and the following passage caught me:

> Woe to you, blind guides! You say, "If anyone swears by the temple, it means nothing; but anyone who swears by the gold of the temple is bound by that oath." You blind fools! Which is greater: the gold, or the temple that makes the gold sacred? (Matthew 23:16–17).

Which is greater, the gold or the temple that makes the gold sacred? In his commentary on the Book of Matthew, Jean Calvin wrote in response to this passage:

> The Jews had more reverence for the gold of the temple, and for the sacred offerings, than for the temple and the altar. But the sacredness of the offerings depended on

the temple and the altar, and was only something inferior and accessory.[6]

I am afraid many of us are becoming much like the Pharisees, placing more honor on the gold (defending marriage, religious freedom, the right to refuse), than on accurately representing the heart of the One who made marriage. It is my concern that in our efforts to fight for righteousness we are obscuring the whole of God's character. I think this is happening because some in the Christian community have created a false dichotomy for believers, stating that there is no way to maintain the integrity of your conviction and conscience while also honoring the law—whether that be in issuing licenses or providing a service at a gay wedding.

Like so many things in the Christian life, the truth seems to lie in the tension: truth and love together. In the Kim Davis scenario and others like it, I don't see a whole lot of love or respect being displayed. In fact, it feels like the greatest concern is not for the advancement of the Kingdom of God, but rather the preservation of rights. In my opinion, that concern is severely out of balance.

Please do not misunderstand me. I *am* concerned about religious liberty. I *am* concerned about the direction our nation and world are headed. I *am* concerned about the growing hostility toward Christianity. And yet, those issues are all secondary for me. My primary concern is not that I might have to offer a service for a marriage that is recognized by our government but contrary to my faith. My greatest concern is this: In all I do and in all my interactions, am I

---

[6] Jean Calvin, "Matthew 23," *Commentary on a Harmony of the Evangelists Matthew, Mark, and Luke*, William Pringle, Trans. (Grand Rapids, MI: Eerdmans, 1965).

displaying the most accurate representation of the gospel, Christ's character, and God's heart?

And yet that can easily become a secondary concern. While writing this book, I became aware of a bill up for consideration in California. This bill would classify any business involving sexual-orientation-change efforts as fraudulent. This impacts more than counseling and therapy; it means someone like myself cannot share my personal testimony at a conference or sell a book with my testimony in it. Essentially, ministry to individuals struggling with their sexual identity would be illegal.

I am deeply, deeply troubled by this. I am compelled to speak out. I do not believe for one moment that the Church should do nothing about this. But I also believe that whatever our response, it *must* honor and reflect the heart of Jesus.

In *The Weight of Glory*, C.S. Lewis wrote this haunting and convicting passage:

> It is a serious thing to live in a society of possible gods and goddesses, to remember that the dullest most uninteresting person you can talk to may one day be a creature which, if you saw it now, you would be strongly tempted to worship, or else a horror and a corruption such as you now meet, if at all, only in a nightmare. All day long we are, in some degree helping each other to one or the other of these destinations. It is in the light of these overwhelming possibilities, it is with the awe and the circumspection proper to them, that we should conduct all of our dealings with one another, all friendships, all loves, all play, all politics. There are no ordinary people. You have never talked to a mere mortal. Nations, cultures, arts, civilizations—these are mortal, and their life is to ours as the life of a gnat. But it is

immortals whom we joke with, work with, marry, snub, and exploit—immortal horrors or everlasting splendors.[7]

My goal when interacting with others is to create the fewest obstacles to God. This does not mean I water down the truth of Scripture or soft-sell sin or avoid difficult confrontations. But it does mean the way I interact with those who are not living lives submitted to the lordship of Christ or those who oppose the work and Word of God, should be as winsome as possible—even while I hold honestly and openly to my convictions. Remember, sinners were not repelled by Christ's righteousness; in fact, they were *drawn* to Him. He was called the friend of sinners. In contrast, the religious Pharisees were most offended by Jesus's words and actions.

Jesus engaged with those caught in sin. Yes, He called them to repentance, but He saved His harshest tones for the self-righteous Pharisees—not the immoral, broken, deceived, and carnal. With those people—the ones labeled sinners—He ate, He served, He touched, He drank, He laughed, He related, He loved—and He spoke truth, graciously calling them to surrender their lives to a Father who was ready to forgive and transform them. That's the kind of winsome I'm talking about.

I believe we can engage publicly with these issues in a way that resembles how Jesus did—not just by standing up for the truth from a pharisaical position of judgement.

We would all do well to ask ourselves: Does the way I live out and communicate my convictions about marriage, sexuality, and the holiness of God help people move closer

---

[7] C.S. Lewis, "The Weight of Glory," *The Weight of Glory and Other Addresses* (New York: Simon & Schuster, 1996).

to God, or does it create additional barriers and push people further away Him?

In their book *Untamed,* Alan and Debra Hirsch write this about the Pharisees of Jesus' day:

> They were sincere, loved their scriptures, believed in the supernatural, were waiting for the Messiah, were decent and morally upright, were zealous, tithed beyond duty, were "missional," and maintained Israel's identity and tradition in a time of occupation. In many ways they were exemplary religious people. It's not hard to see how they are very much like us! We believe that if we do not read them as ourselves, we miss much of the truth of what Jesus has to say to us, and we will likely commit precisely the same sins that are associated with them. It is a problem every religious person encounters in life. Religious people get very fussy about "things" and then become coercive about it. If we are not careful, we can end up defending truths and at the same time miss Truth—just like the Pharisees. It's all about how we INHABIT our beliefs and how we allow the power of our beliefs to inhabit or mold us.[8]

I am deeply concerned about what is happening in our culture. I greatly appreciate and depend upon the freedom to exercise and proclaim my faith and my testimony. I am deeply disturbed by the cultural trend to demonize, marginalize, and villainize people of faith because of their convictions regarding marriage and sexuality. I am also deeply concerned and disturbed by the shaming that I have seen—and have personally experienced—by others in the Christian community for not responding to the issues of

---

[8] Alan and Debra Hirsch, *Untamed: Reactivating a Missional Form of Discipleship* (Ada, MI: Baker Books, 2010), 223.

religious freedom as my top priority and instead focusing on the relational tensions and realities that surround these issues. This is troublesome.

Here are a few difficult questions I suggest we all contend with:

- Do we as Christians care more about our right to religious liberty than we do about revealing the heart of God to those around us?

- Do we care that there is one man and one woman in every marriage more than we care that the convictions we have about what makes a holy, healthy, and Christ-revealing marriage actually mold and manifest themselves in our own marriages and the marriages in our faith community?

- Do we care more that we have the protected right not to participate in a same-sex marriage by providing a service (baking a wedding cake, signing a marriage license, etc.), or is it a greater violation of our religion that, in an effort to avoid the former, we misrepresent the heart of God to those around us and push them further away from Him?

- Do we care more that our ability to speak redemptively about sexuality is being threatened than we do that the manner, tone, and content of the words we *do* speak remain firmly redemptive and inhabited with the heart of Jesus?

I believe we can—respectfully, gently, and wisely—work to preserve religious freedoms. And we must. But I also wholeheartedly believe this should be secondary to loving well. And if we *are* to love well, in a way that accurately represents the character of God, we will have to learn how to show respect and deference to those we may profoundly disagree with—even those who are attacking us. Paul wrote to his spiritual son, Timothy:

Don't have anything to do with foolish and stupid arguments, because you know they produce quarrels. And the Lord's servant must not be quarrelsome but must be kind to everyone, able to teach, not resentful. Opponents must be gently instructed, in the hope that God will grant them repentance leading them to a knowledge of the truth, and that they will come to their senses and escape from the trap of the devil, who has taken them captive to do his will (2 Timothy 2:23–26 NIV).

We need to examine our hearts. We need to examine whether an issue is actually a violation of our conscience or religious freedoms or whether it is just something we'd rather not do. We are going to have to learn not just to defend a holy view of sexuality and marriage, but also *inhabit* it—all while maintaining an attitude that reflects the character of the One who established holy matrimony. In short, through our speech and in our actions, we must learn to accurately reflect the heart and character of Jesus.

Are we there yet?

Not quite. But we can get there. And it would help if the people on the stage were singing more beautifully—if this whole special music number wasn't so painful to sit through. And yet, even though I wish all these things, the lesson from one-too-many bad Sandi Patty renditions still rings true: I absolutely cannot judge the heart of Kim Davis or any other player in this unfolding drama. I don't know if she is a gracious individual who truly grieves for the hearts of those caught in sin. I don't know if her decisions are coming from a place of self-righteousness or genuine concern. I don't know her heart. God does.

My prayer is simple: Church, may we please remember that whatever we encounter, the very eternity of the people we interact with may be affected by how we choose to model Christ to them. Let us pray that the Holy Spirit will give us all a greater understanding of how to engage each person and scenario with truth and love, so that whatever our interaction, we help them walk a few steps closer to the arms of the Father. Let us work to never push them farther away.

> If I speak in the tongues of men or of angels, but do not have love, I am only a resounding gong or a clanging cymbal. If I have the gift of prophecy and can fathom all mysteries and all knowledge, and if I have a faith that can move mountains, but do not have love, I am nothing. If I give all I possess to the poor and give over my body to hardship that I may boast, but do not have love, I gain nothing. Love is patient, love is kind. It does not envy, it does not boast, it is not proud. It does not dishonor others, it is not self-seeking, it is not easily angered, it keeps no record of wrongs. Love does not delight in evil but rejoices with the truth. It always protects, always trusts, always hopes, always perseveres. Love never fails. But where there are prophecies, they will cease; where there are tongues, they will be stilled; where there is knowledge, it will pass away. For we know in part and we prophesy in part, but when completeness comes, what is in part disappears. When I was a child, I talked like a child, I thought like a child, I reasoned like a child. When I became a man, I put the ways of childhood behind me. For now we see only a reflection as in a mirror; then we shall see face to face. Now I know in part; then I shall know fully, even as I am fully known. And now these three remain: faith, hope and love. But the greatest of these is love. (1 Corinthians 13 NIV).

Made in the USA
Middletown, DE
28 March 2022

63274514R00096